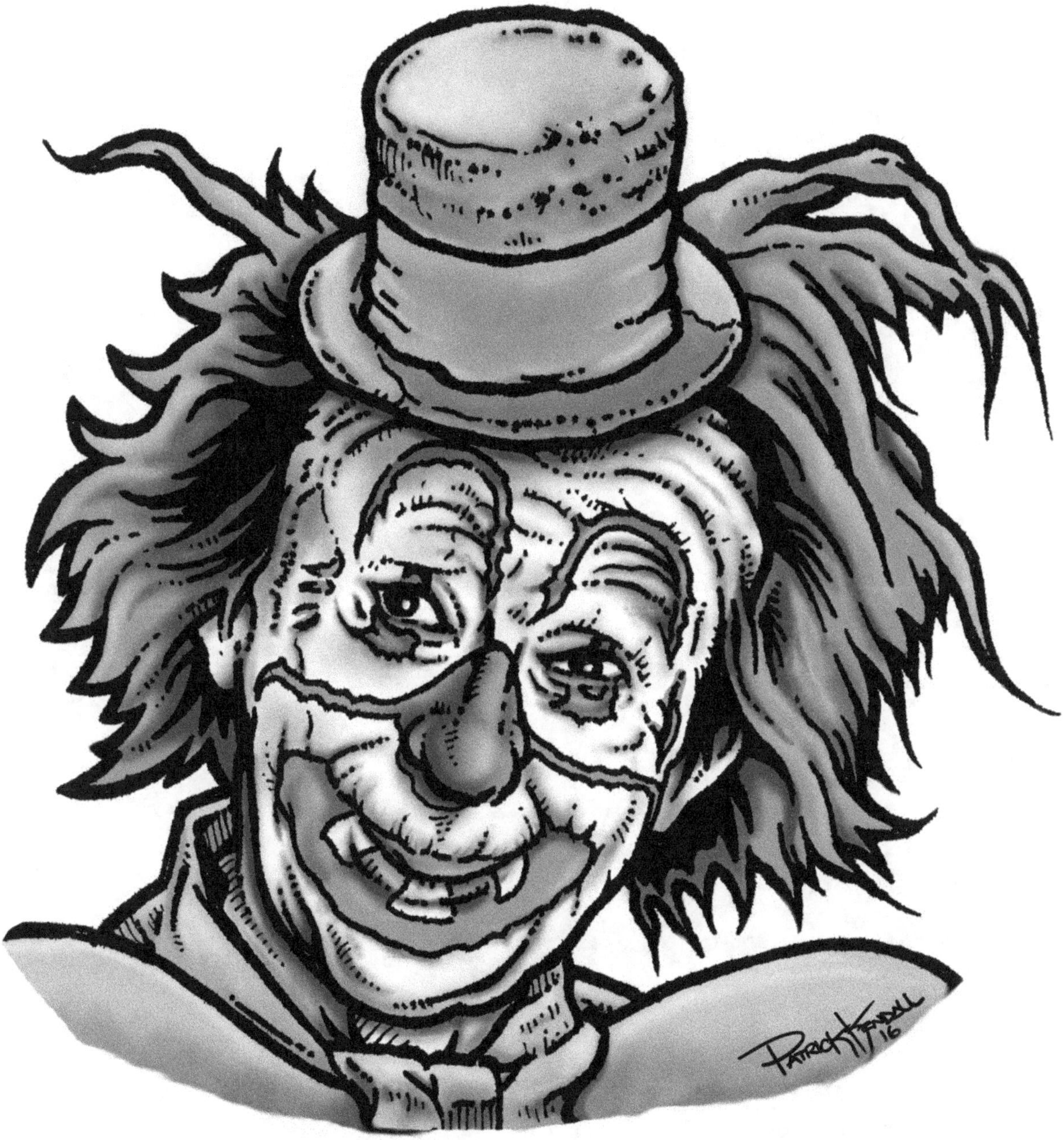

CREEPY CLOWN ADULT COLORING BOOK

Written and Compiled By:
Jordan R. Colton

Cover by:
Patrick Kendall

Copyright © 2016 Jordan Colton
All rights reserved.
ISBN-13: 978-0692648445
ISBN-10: 0692648445

DEDICATION

This coloring book is dedicated to all those that have had a fear of clowns or after going through this coloring book, begins to have a fear of these circus freaks!

INTRODUCTION

Coulrophobia; it is a term that not everyone is aware of, but it is the informal term for a fear of clowns. I honestly believe that most of us these days have an underlying fear of these circus creatures thanks to pop culture. From the popularity of Stephen King's IT in book and film form (played by the legend Tim Curry), to the more recent take from American Horror Story, media has solidified clowns as more foe than friend.

I can remember as a small child going to the circus with my grandfather and being introduced to a clown for the first time. The white pale make-up and exaggerated facial features looked strange to my naïve eyes at first but as they drew closer to me with the sound of their distorted laughter, fear enveloped me and we had to leave the show early to calm me down. It is ironic that a few years later I actually dressed up as a clown for Halloween, despite the unsettling encounter.

Your own experience may have similarities to my own, or may have been even more traumatic. Countless people all over the world have developed the fear of clowns and I believe that it not only originates from fiction but from reality as well. You may have heard of John Wayne Gasey, who in the 1970s was dubbed the "Killer Clown". At the time he was a professional clown that would attend children's parties, and various events in Illinois performing as "Pogo the Clown," a character of his own invention. It was under this pretense that he would lure in his victims, doing as he wished with them and then disposing of their lifeless bodies. A serial killer, he was at large for over six years. When Pogo was finally caught in 1980, he was sentenced to death for 12 of the 33 murders for which he had been convicted, and executed by lethal injection.

"Pogo" became national news and all over the country the suspicion that clowns were not to be trusted continued to grow. Parents wouldn't hire clowns anymore for parties or events, and that fear is made evident in the presence of clowns more commonly in haunted houses than in parties and festive events.

I and the rest of the Horrid Coloring Book team invite you to not only face your Coulrophobia, but to entertain it! Clowns may be something that many fear, but when you are finished with your scary clown coloring book, we'll see who has the last laugh!
Stay Scary and Happy Coloring!

Jordan Colton

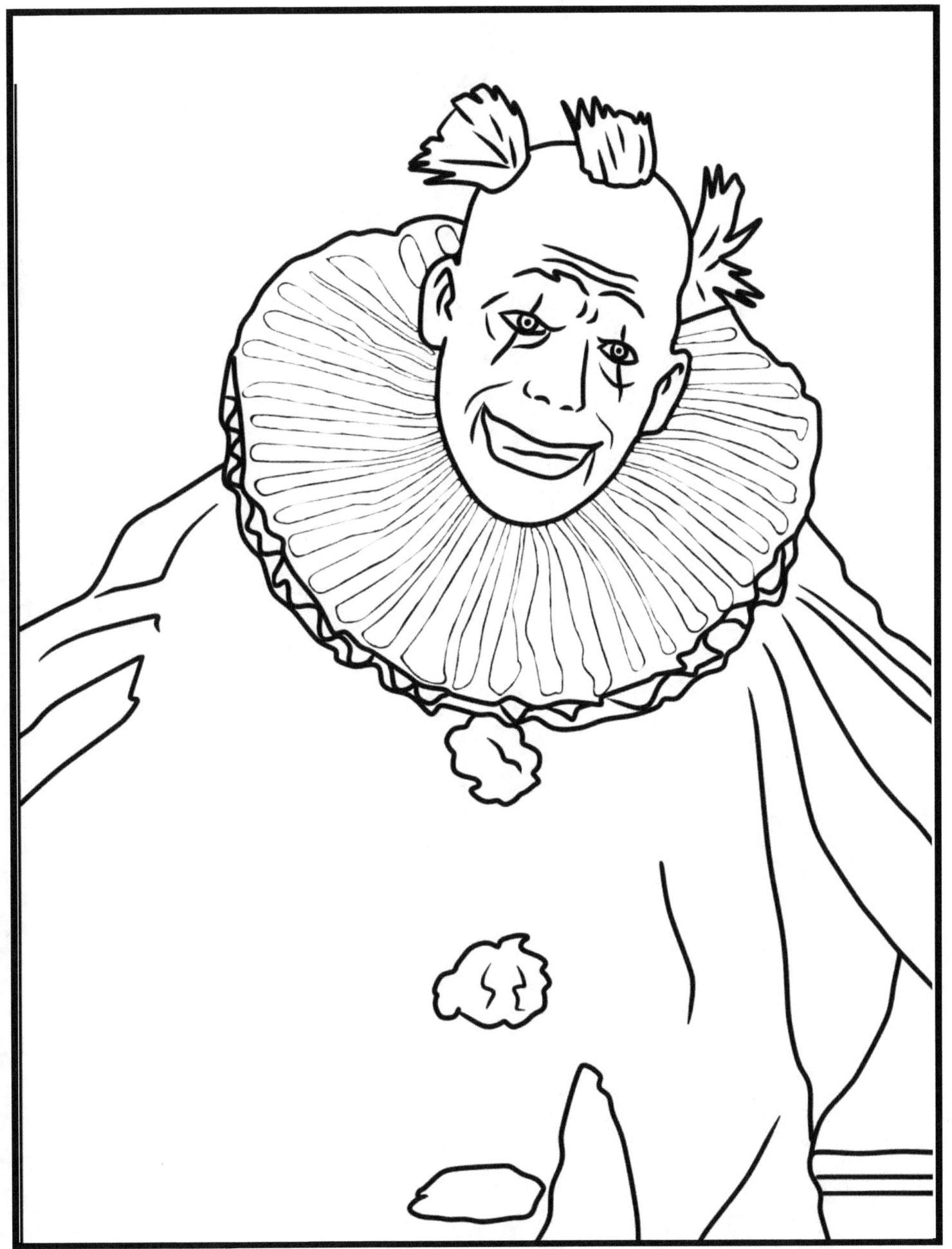

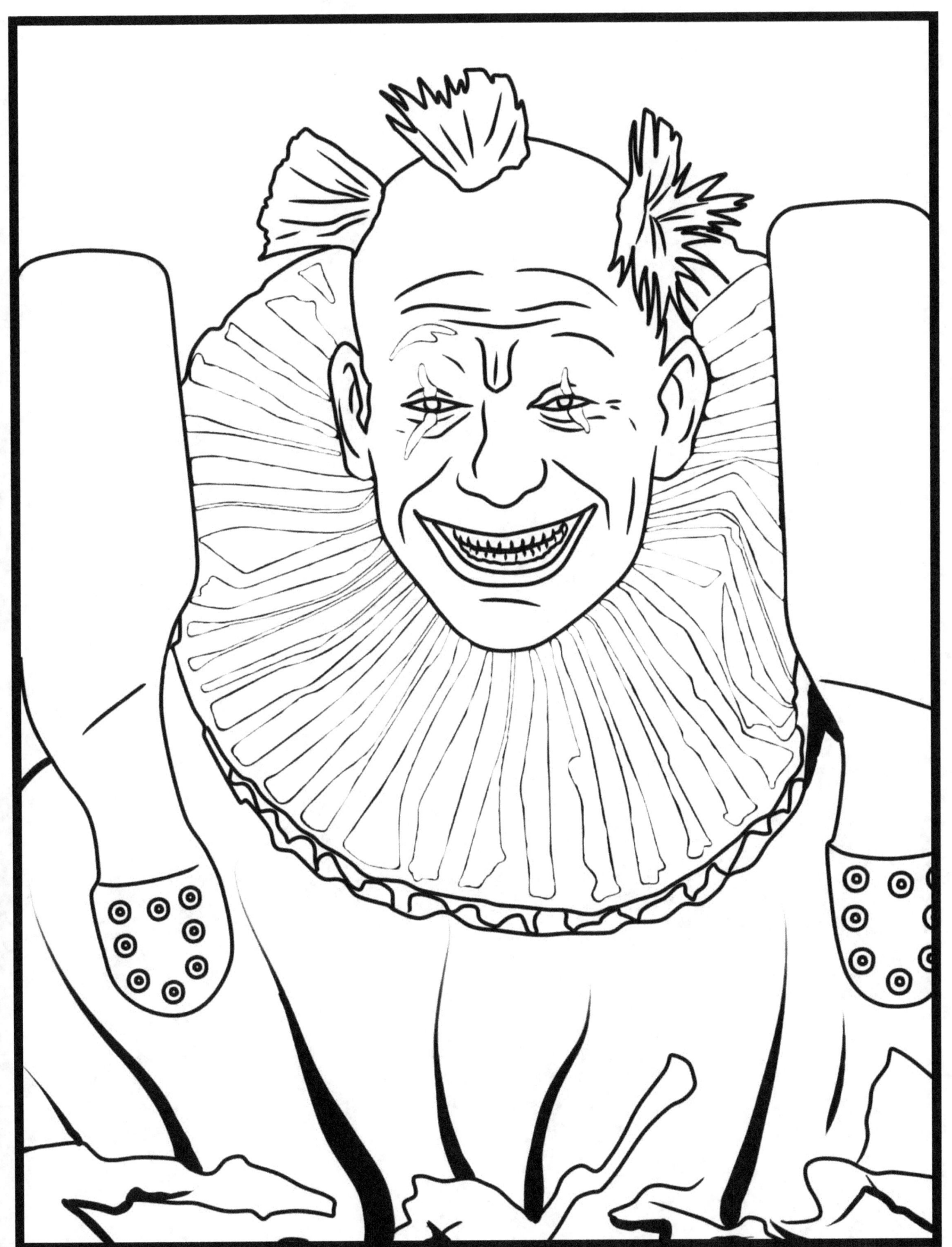

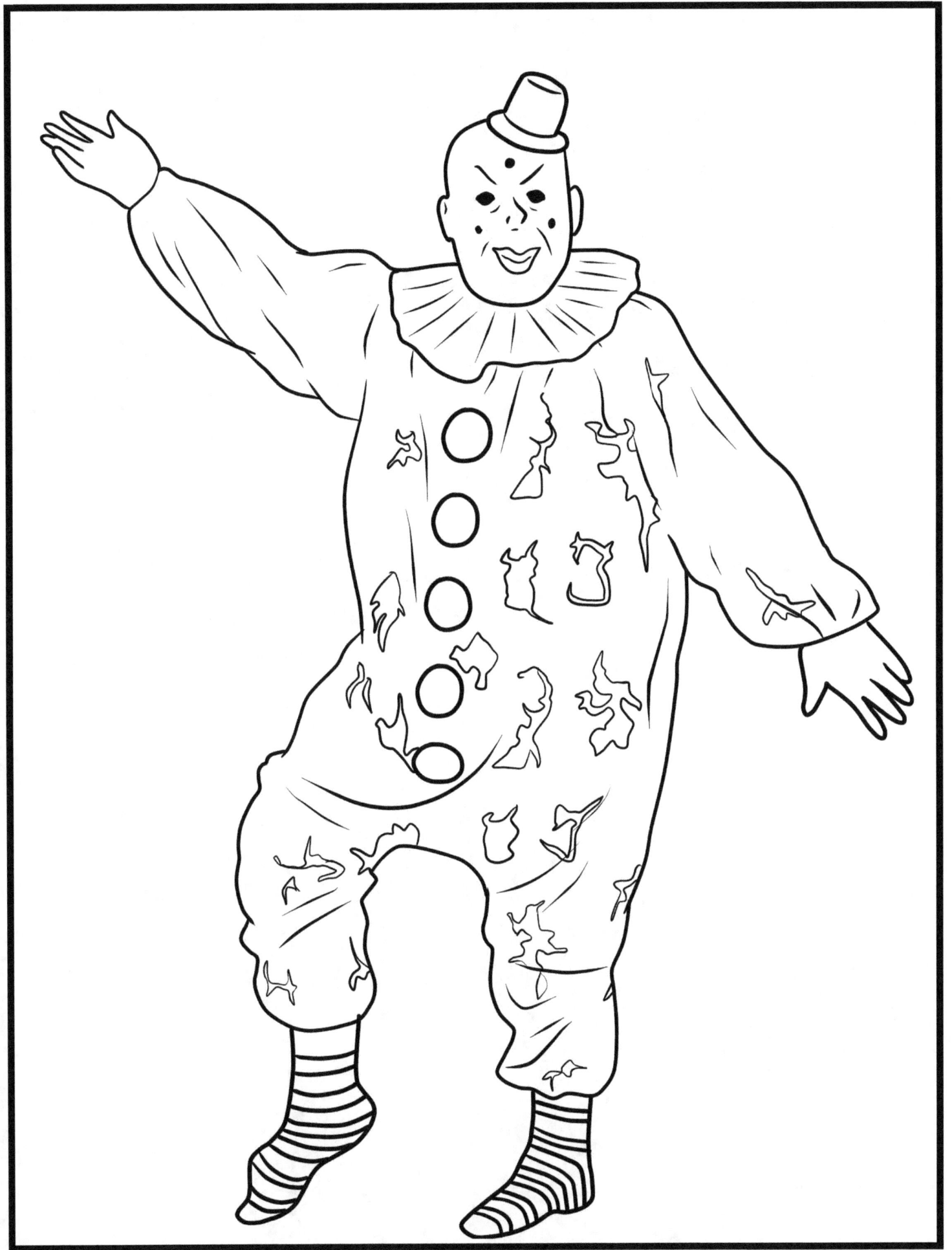

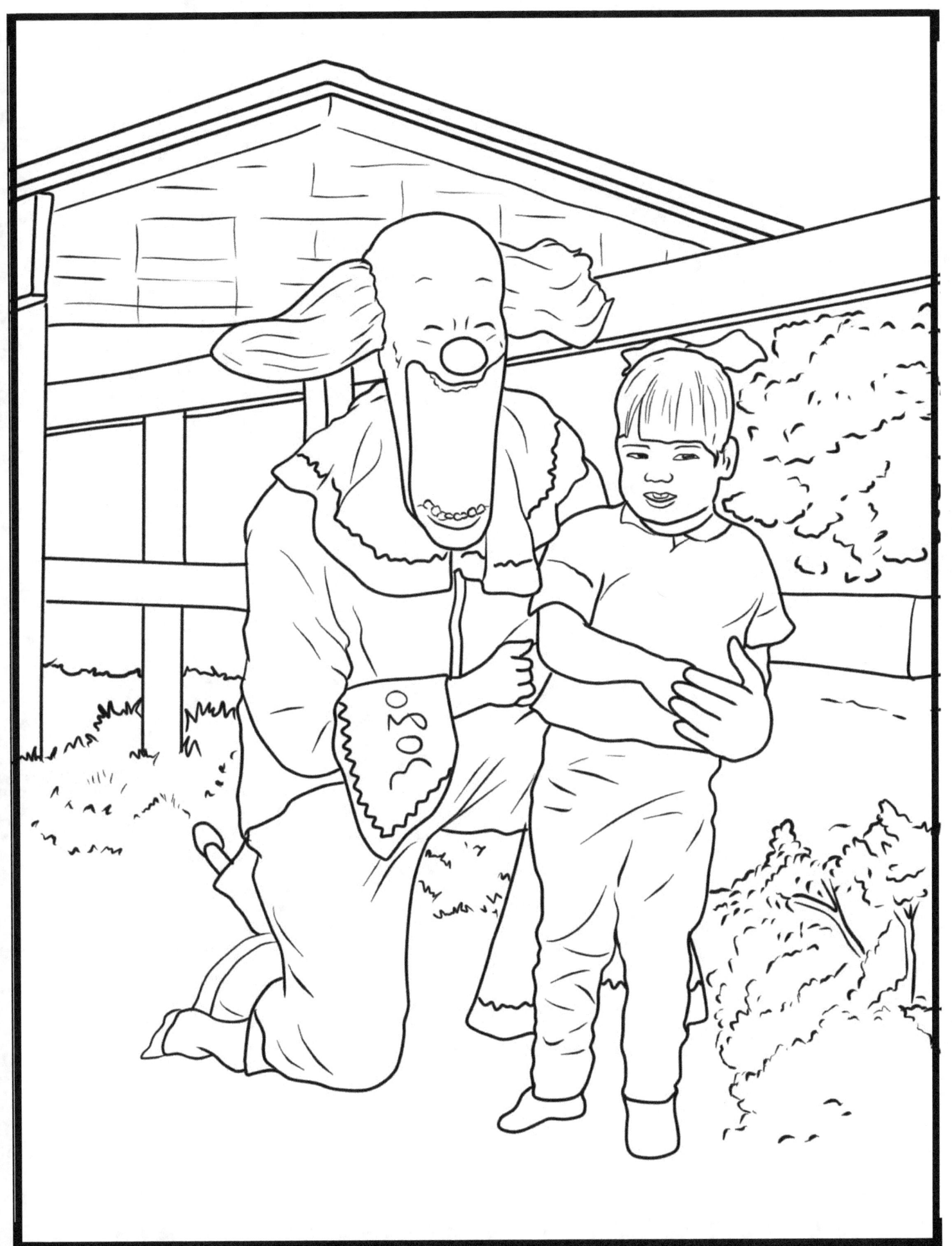

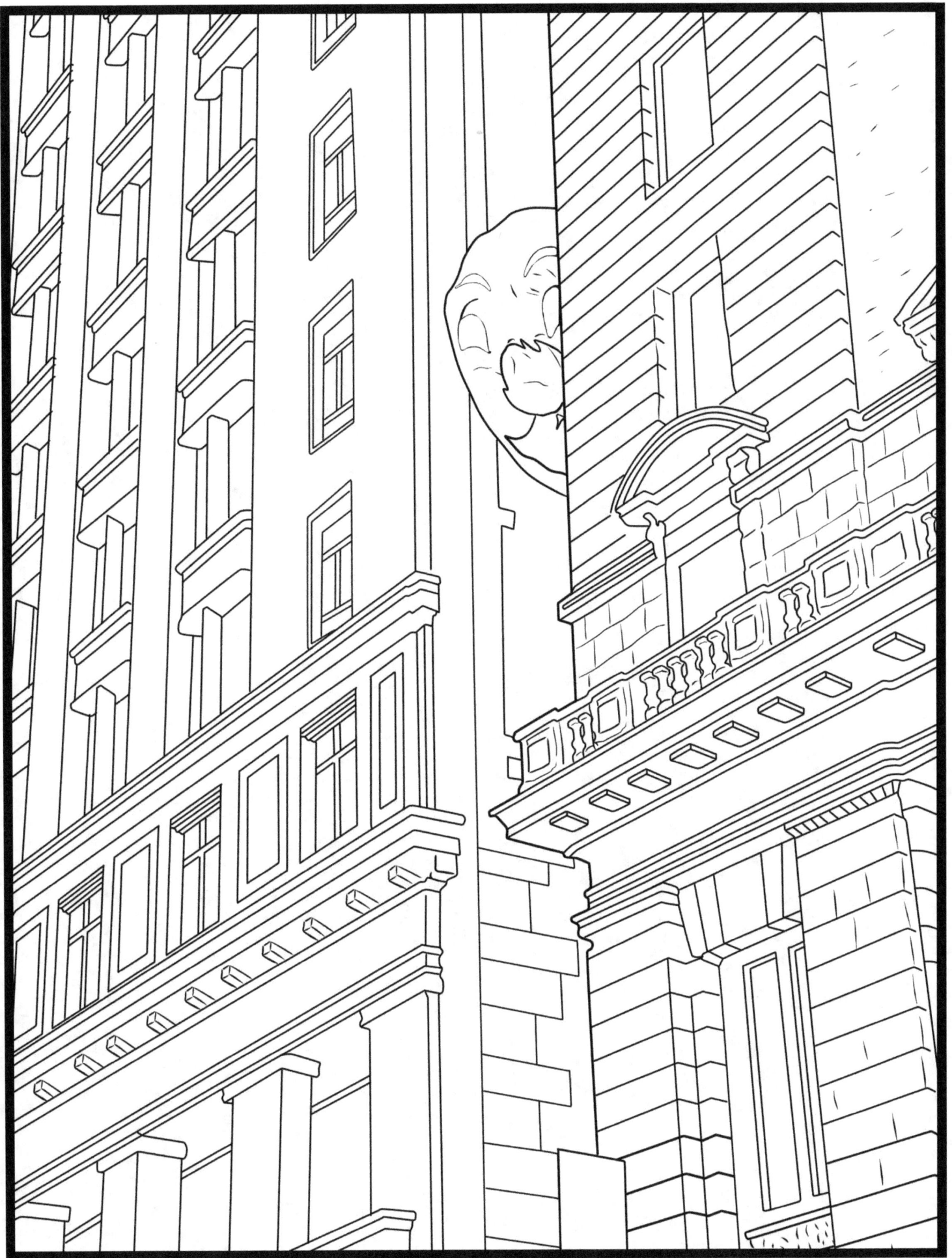

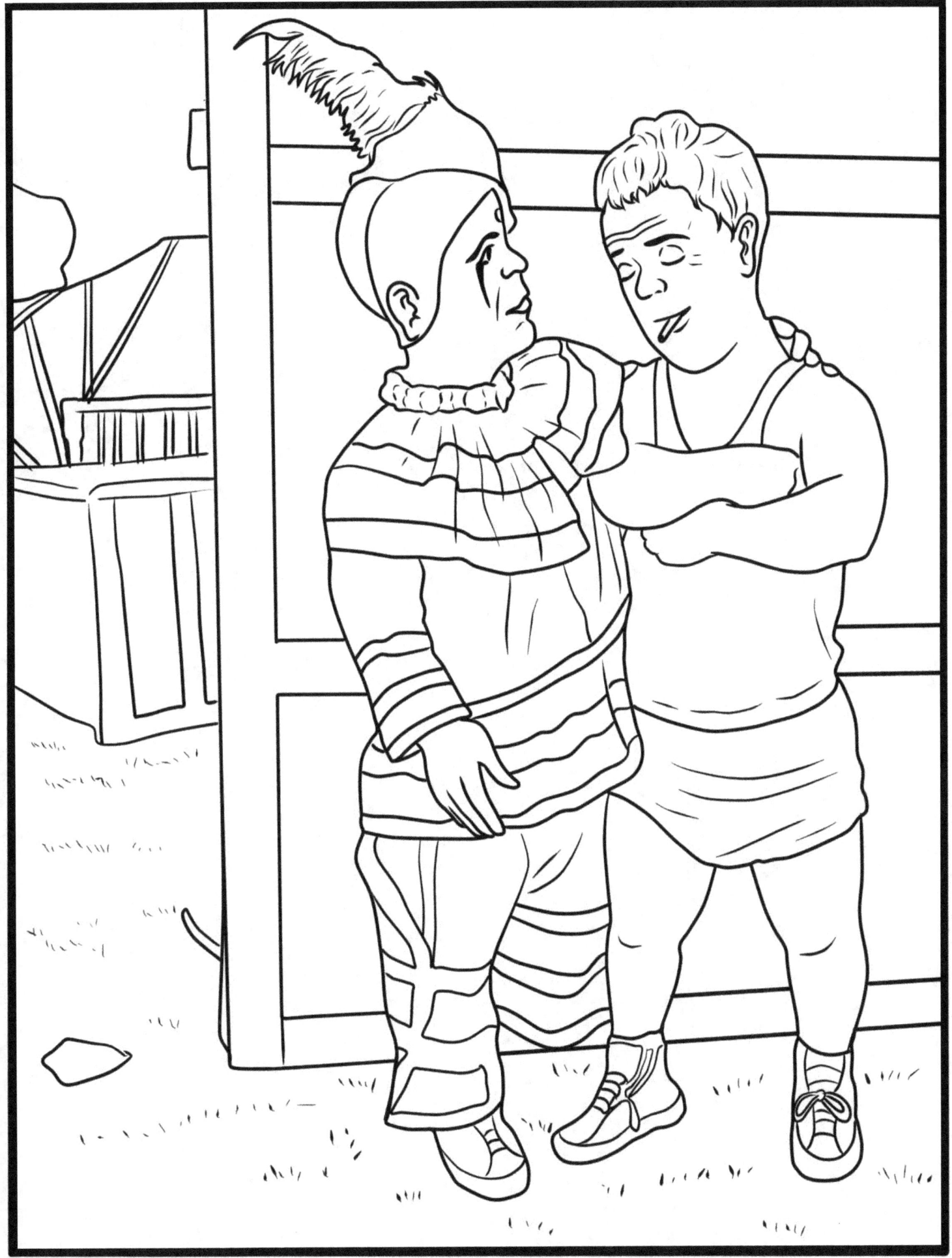

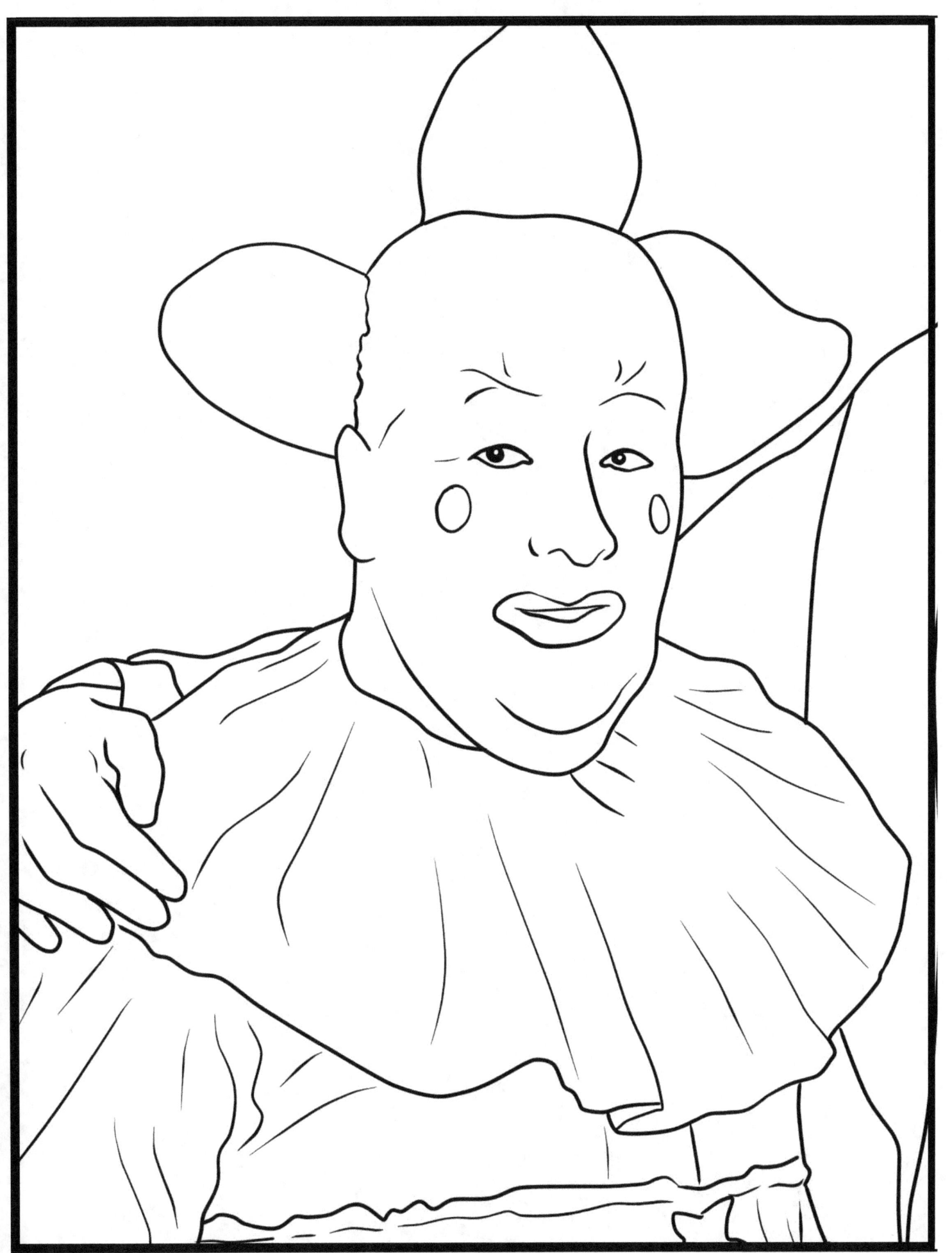

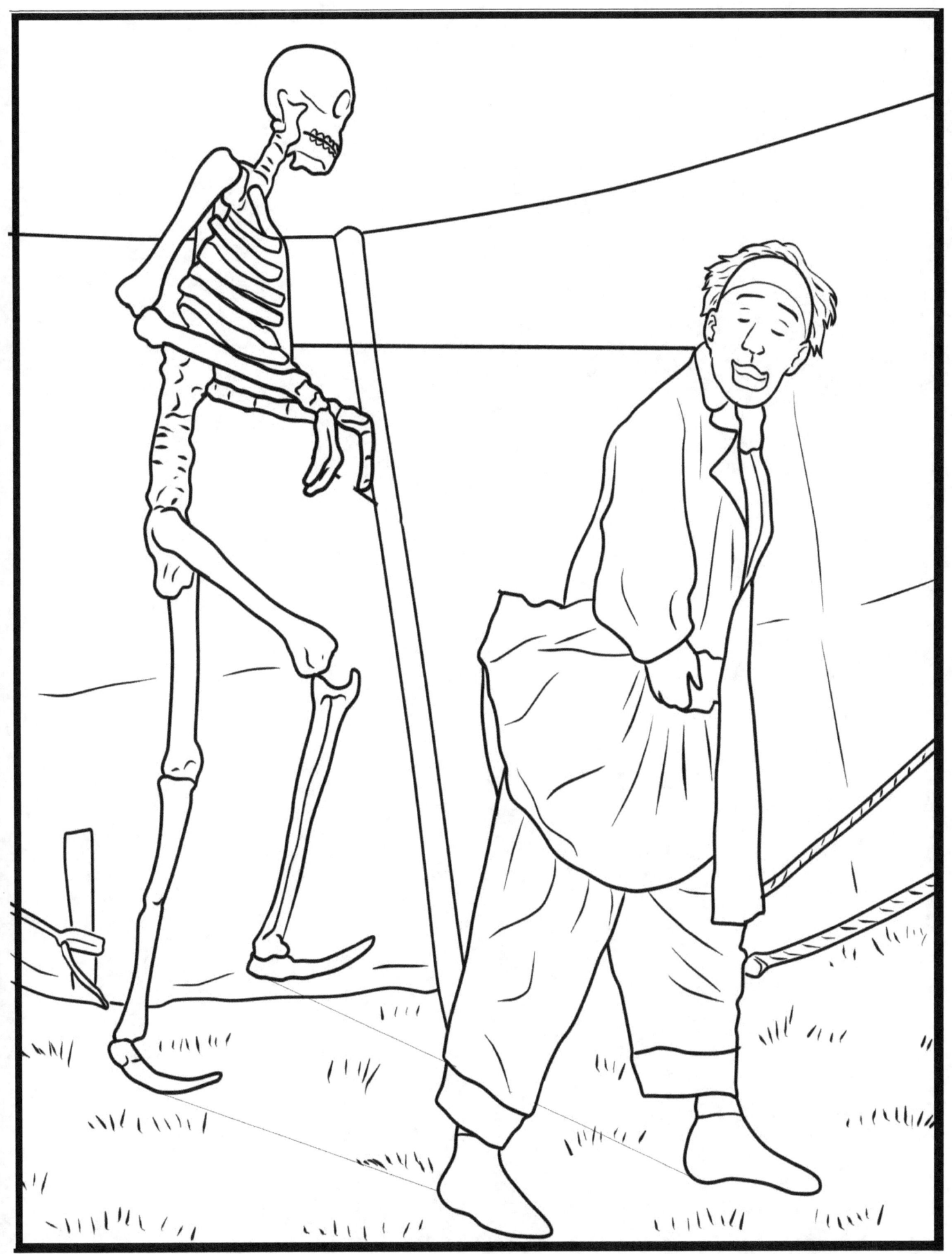

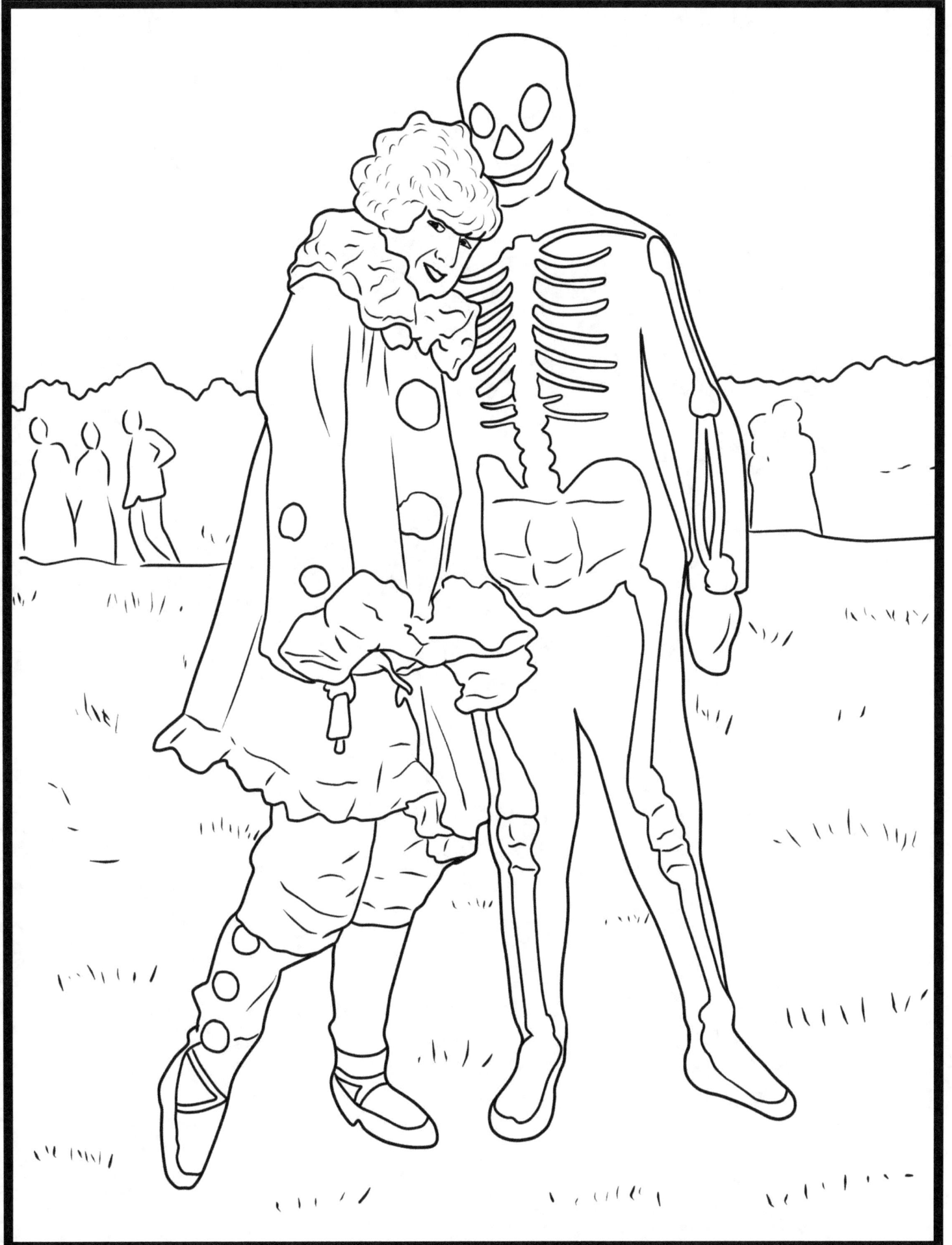

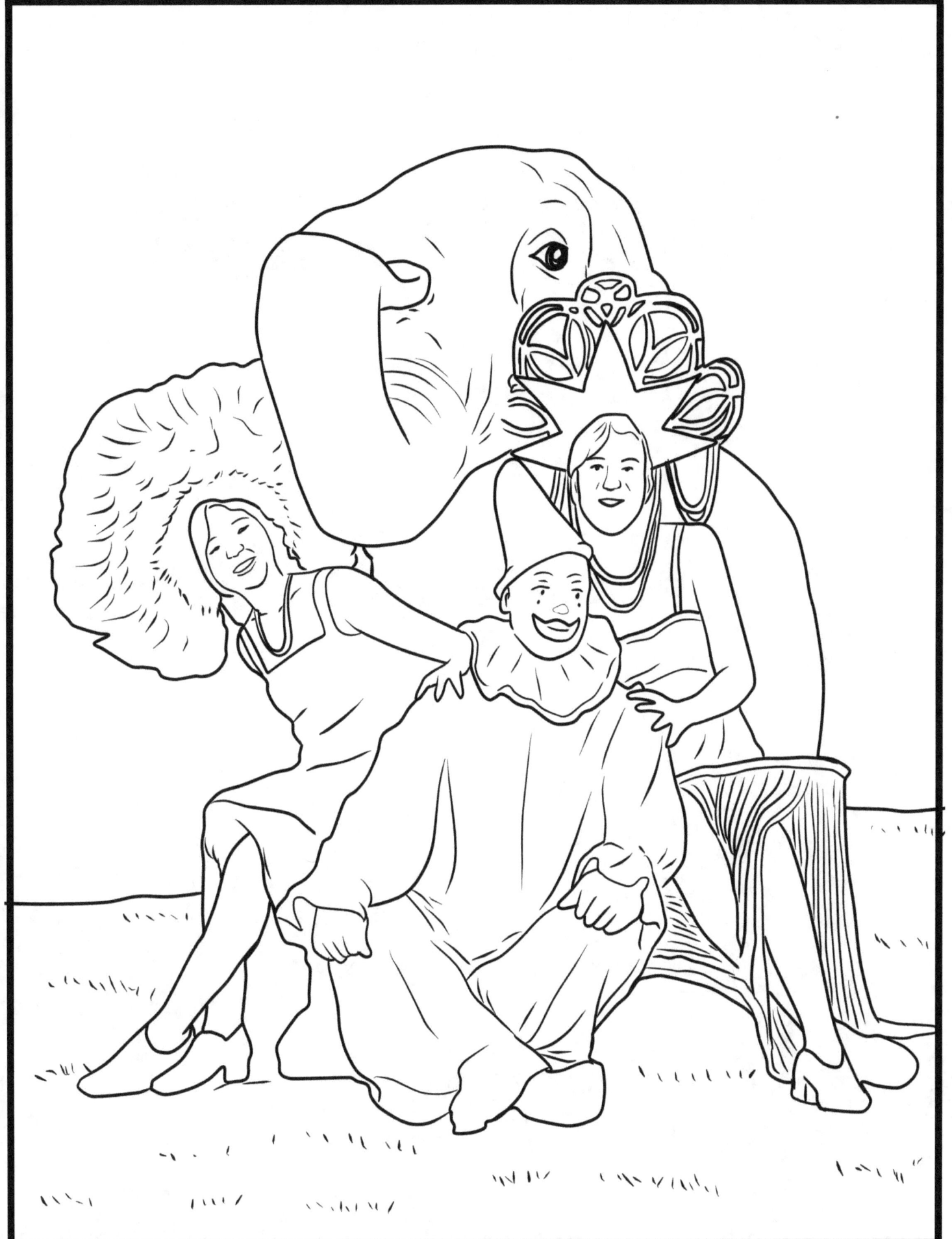

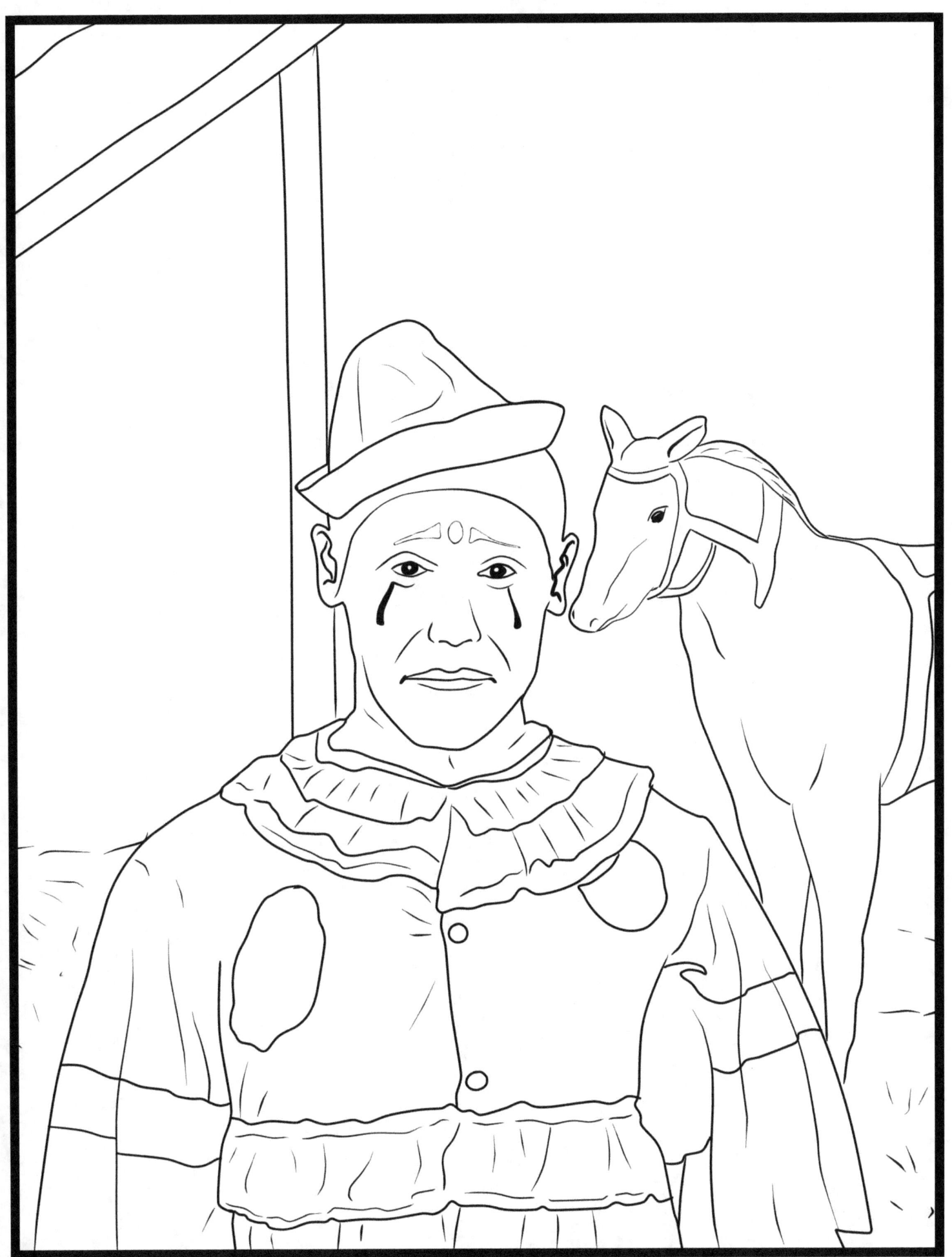

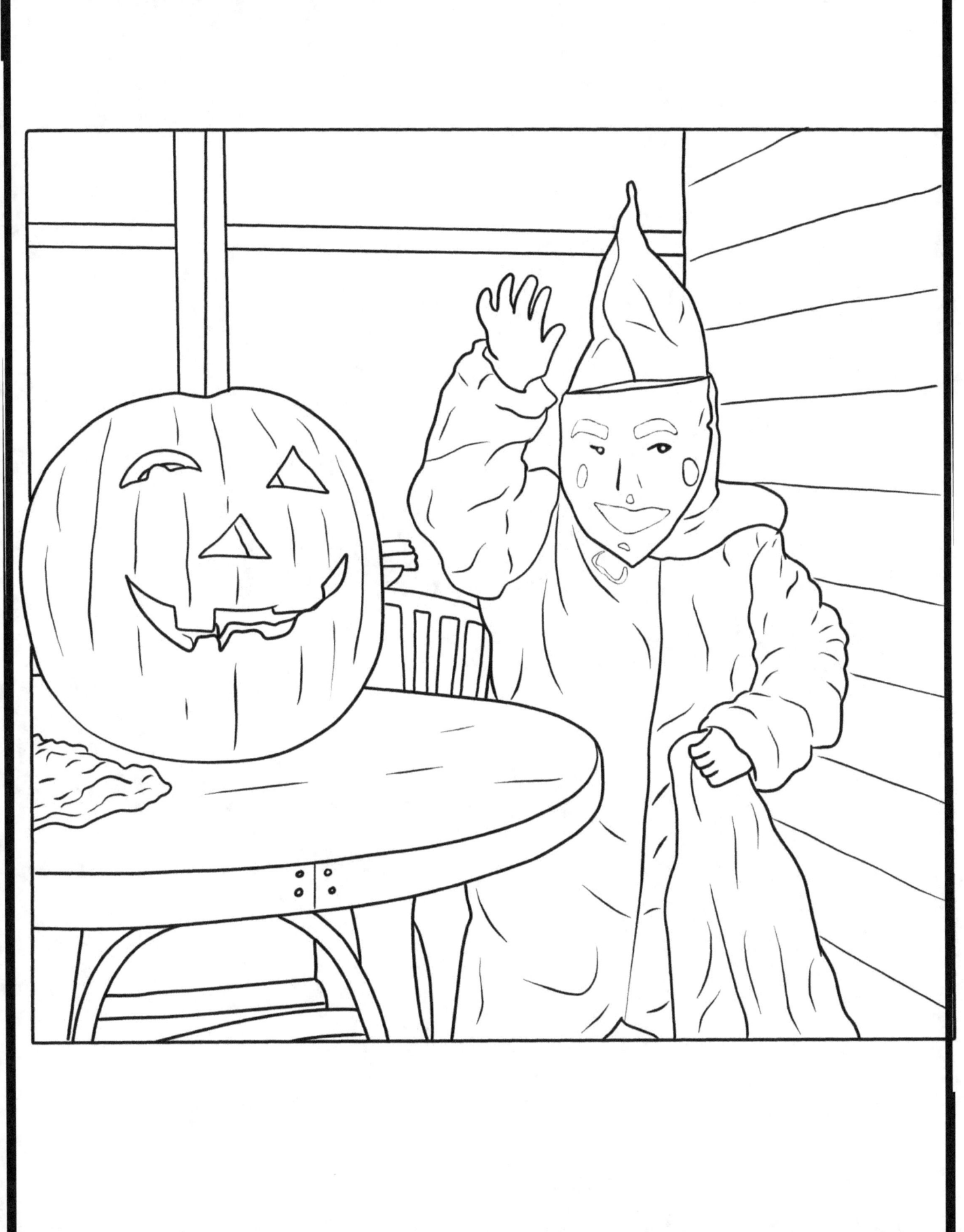

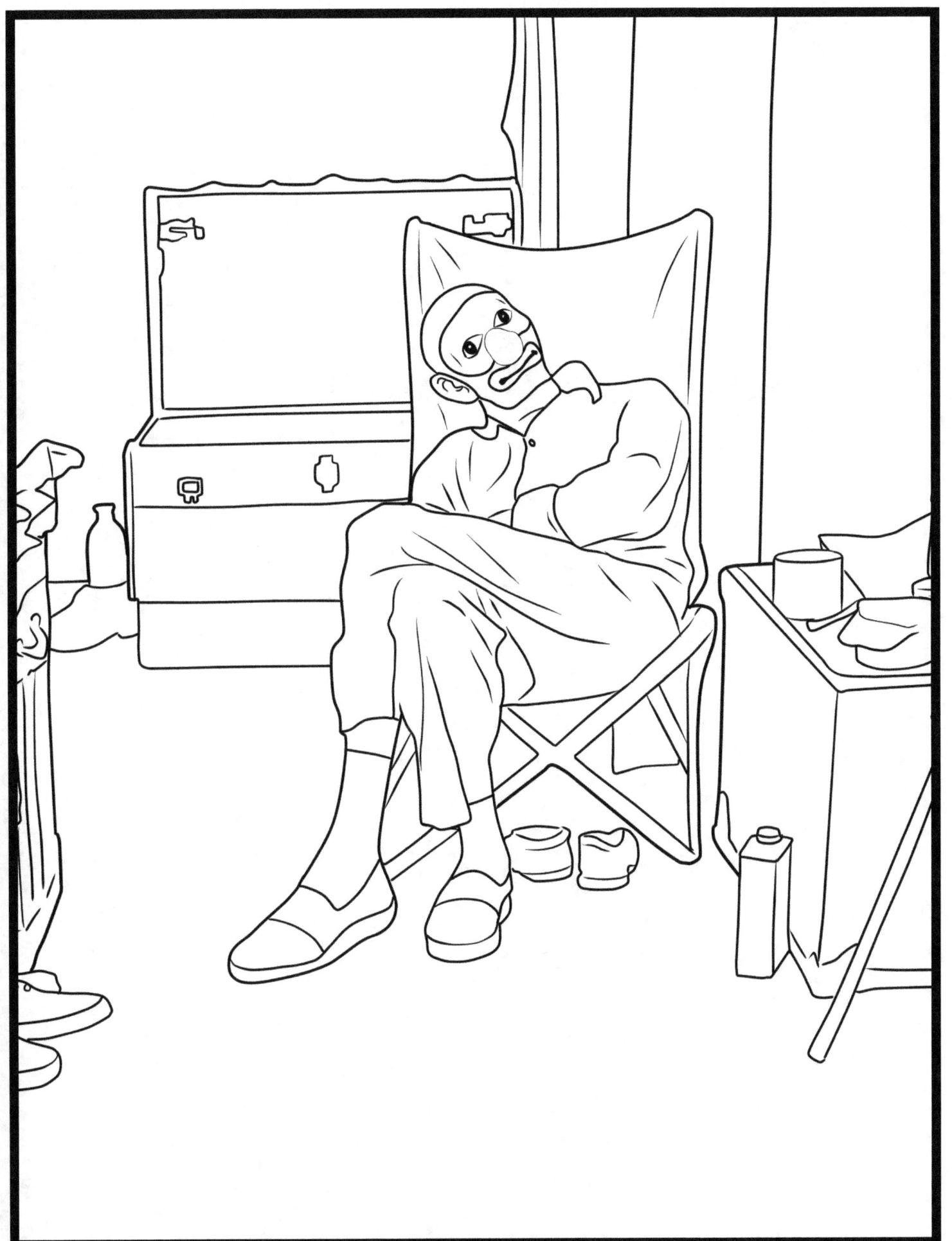

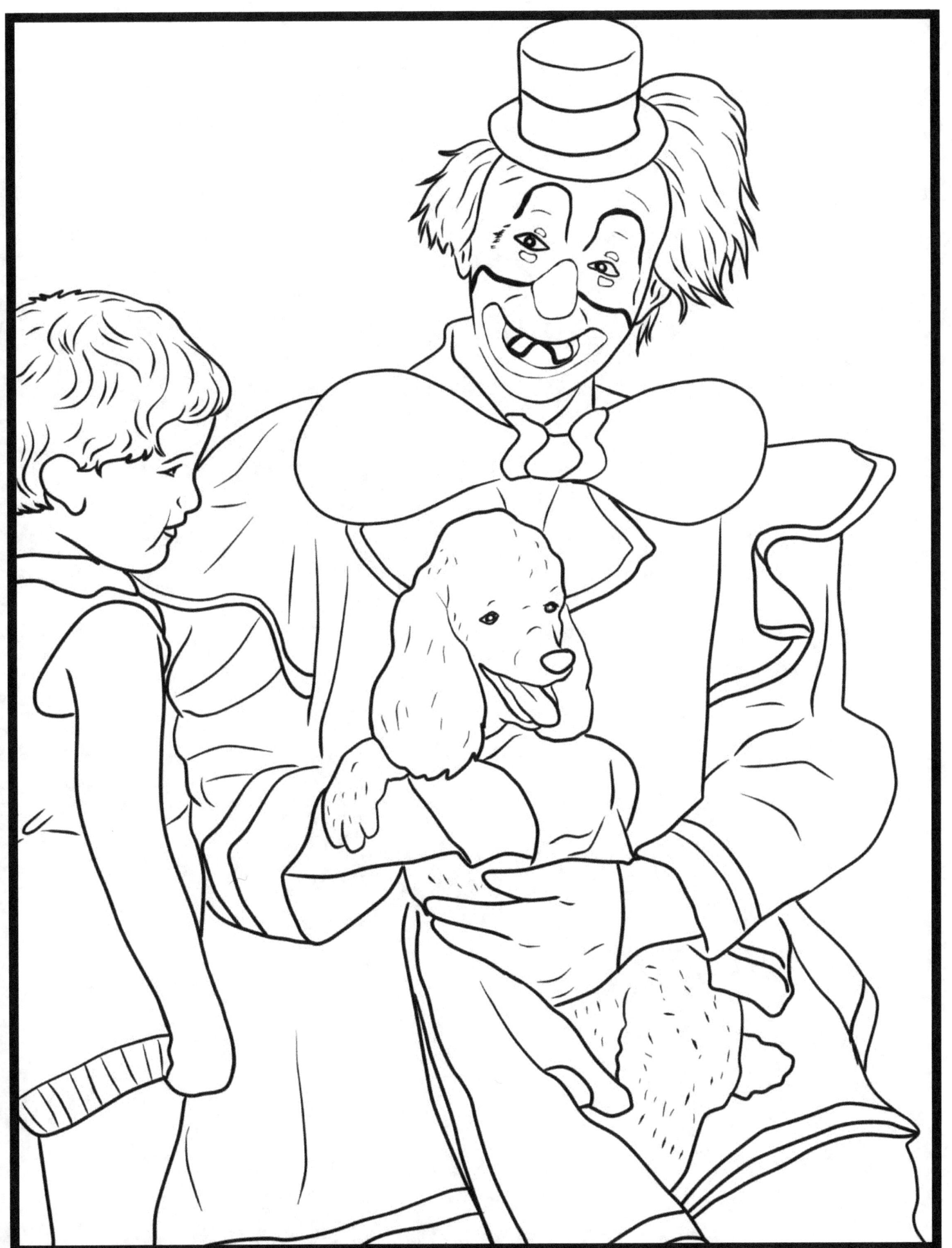

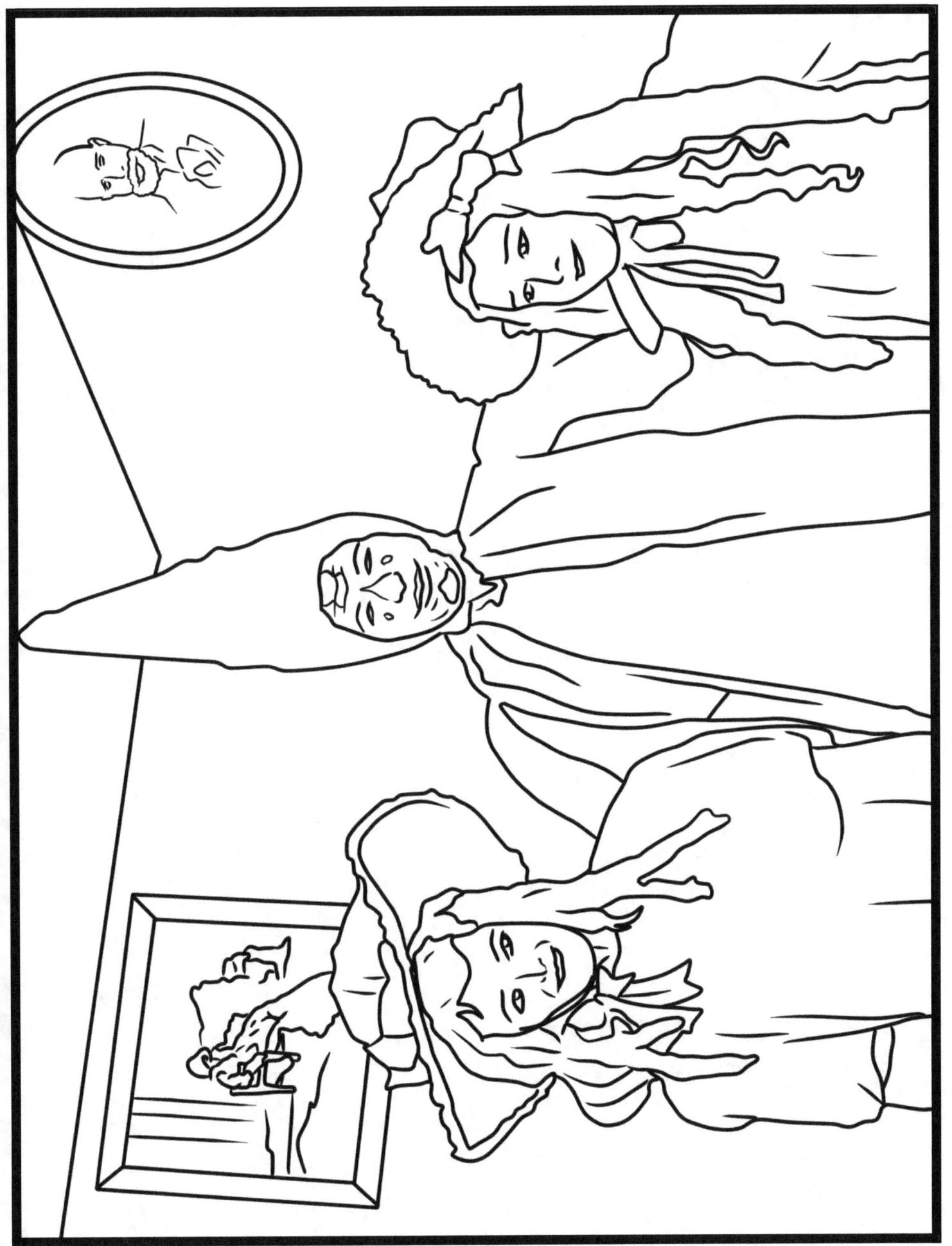

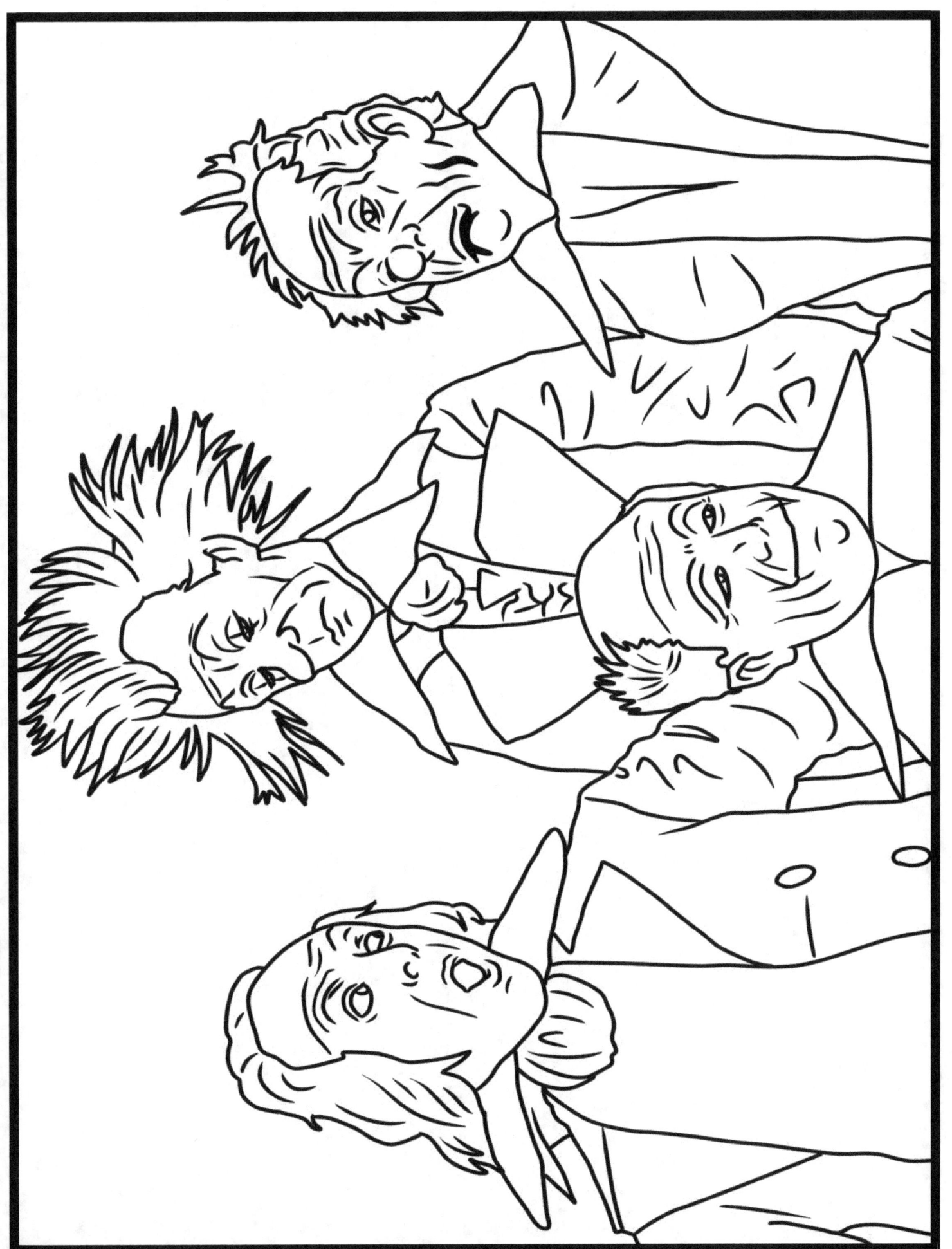

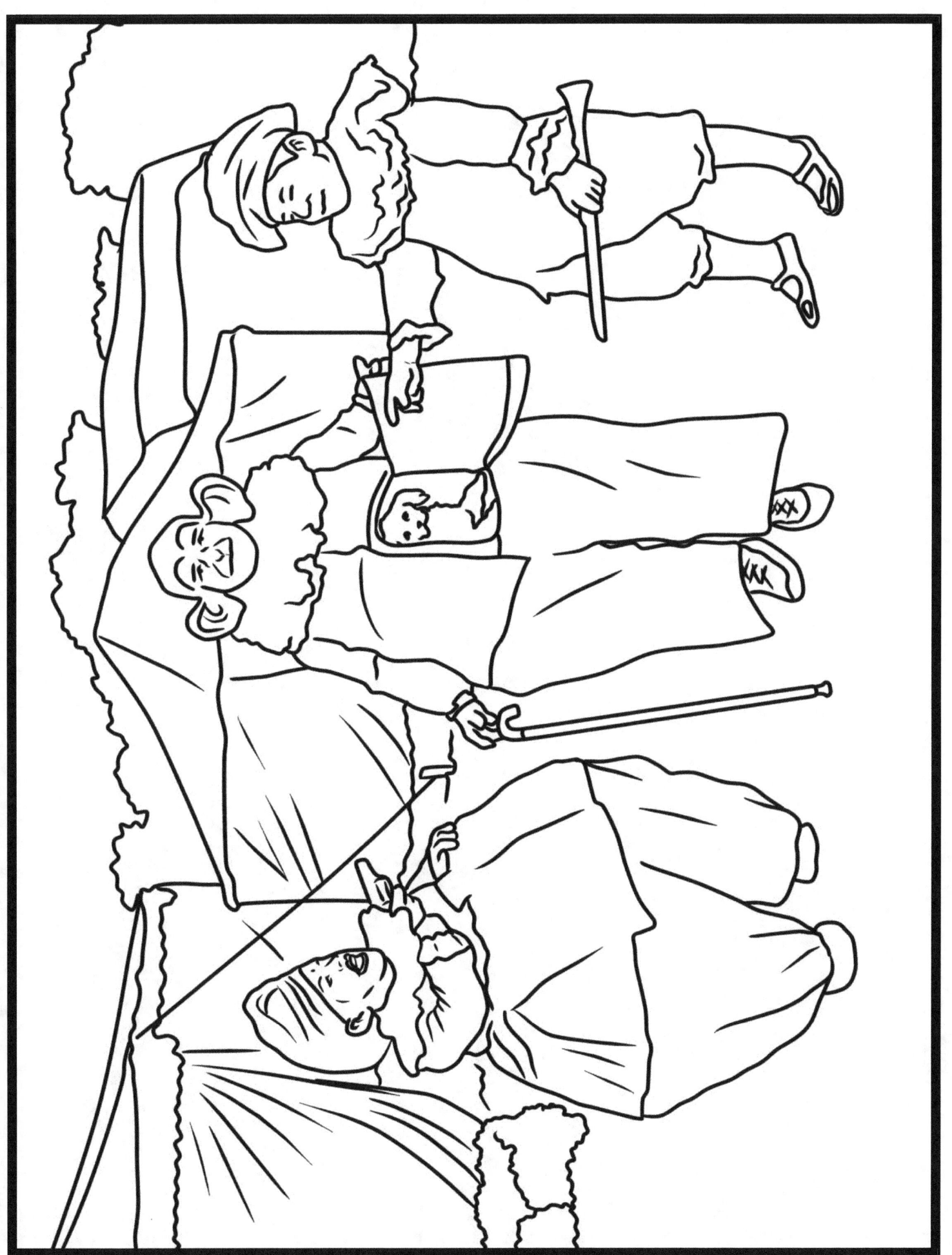

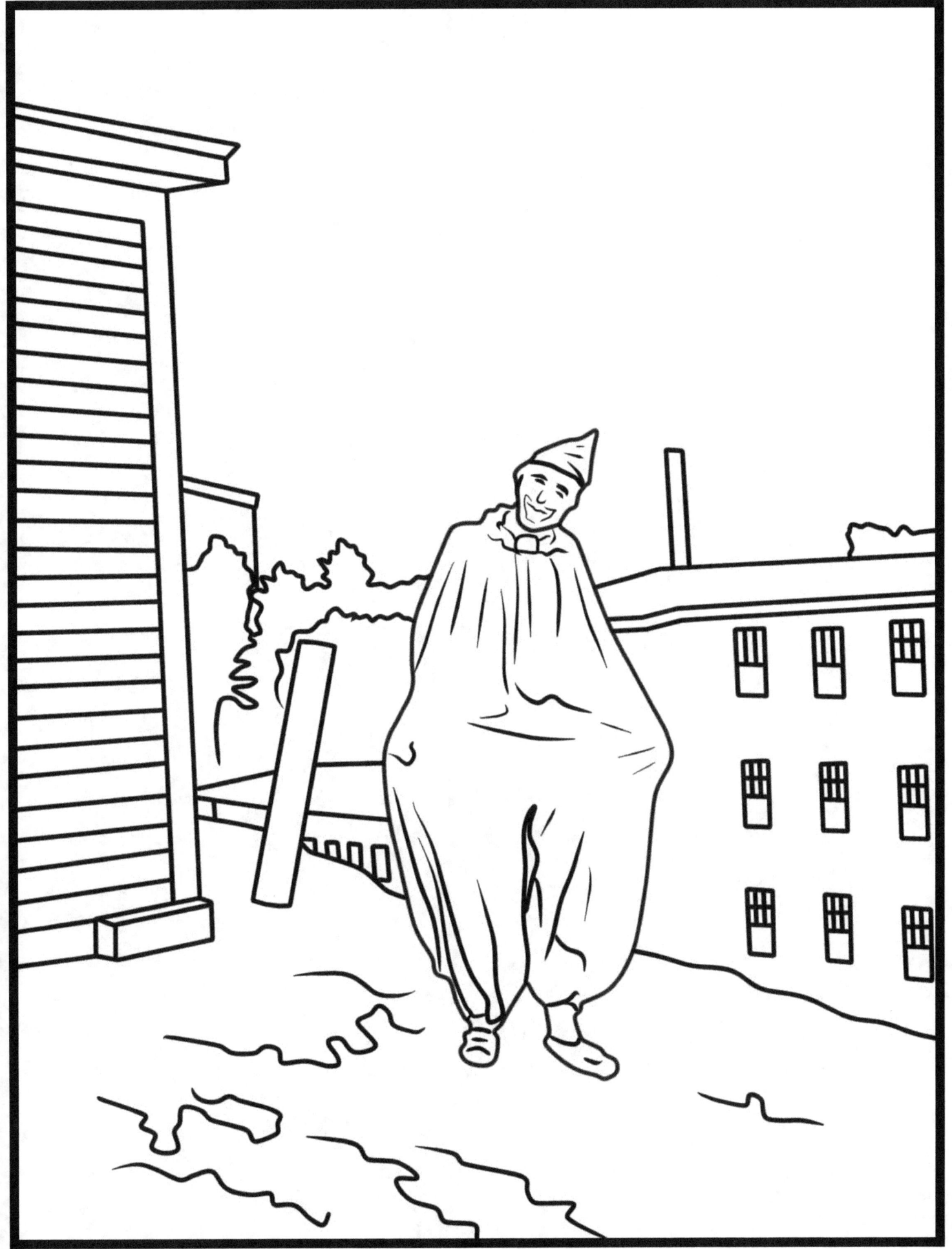

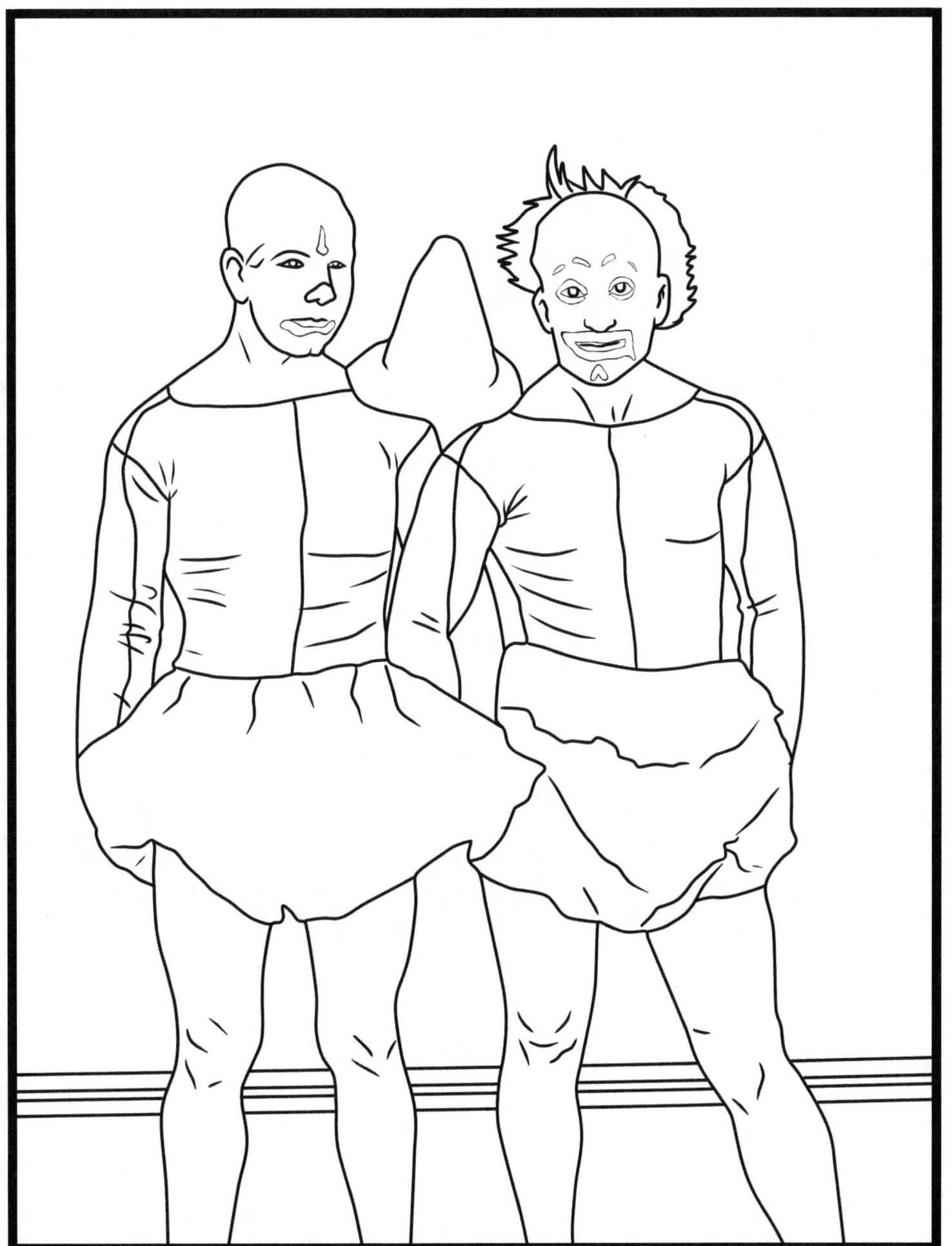

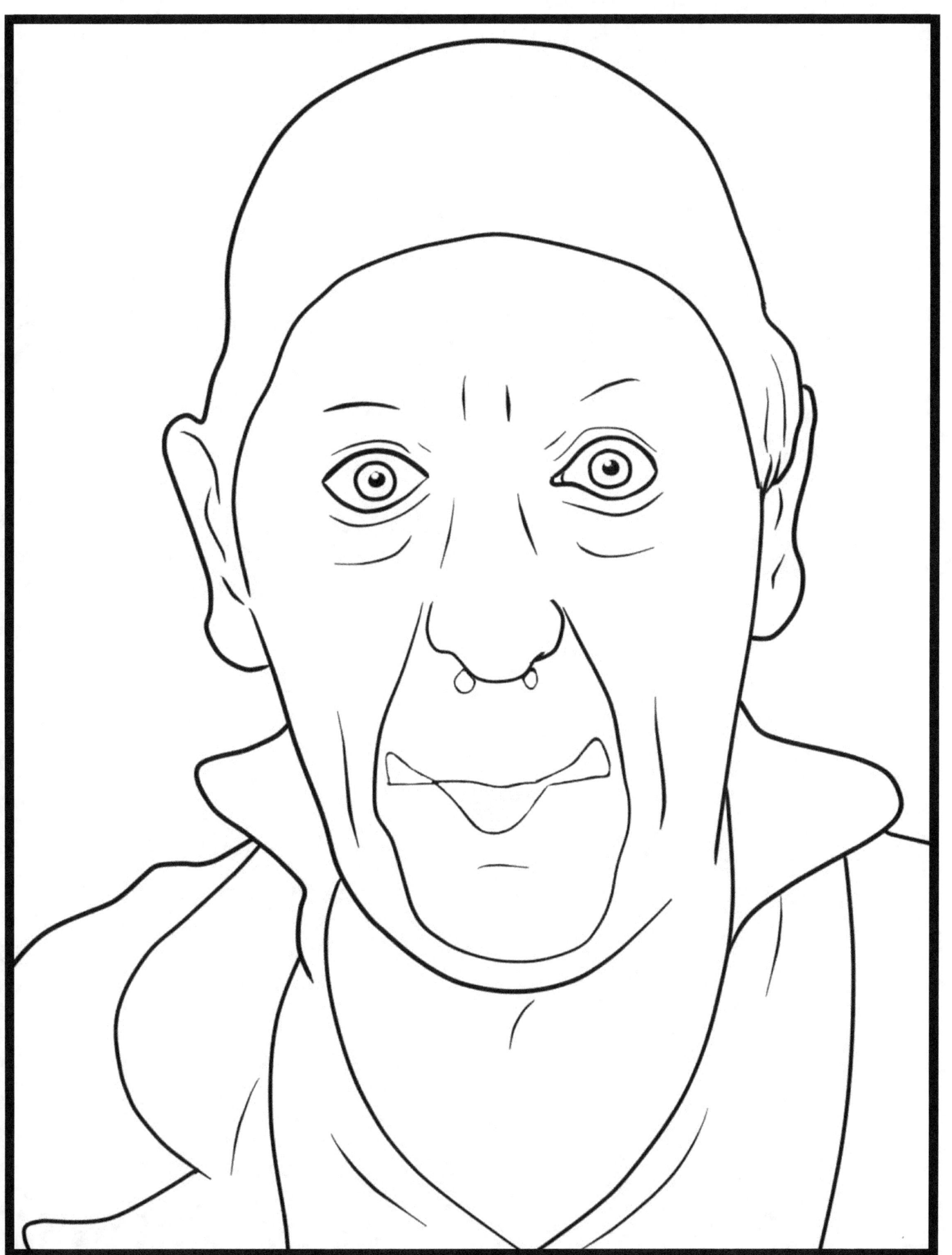

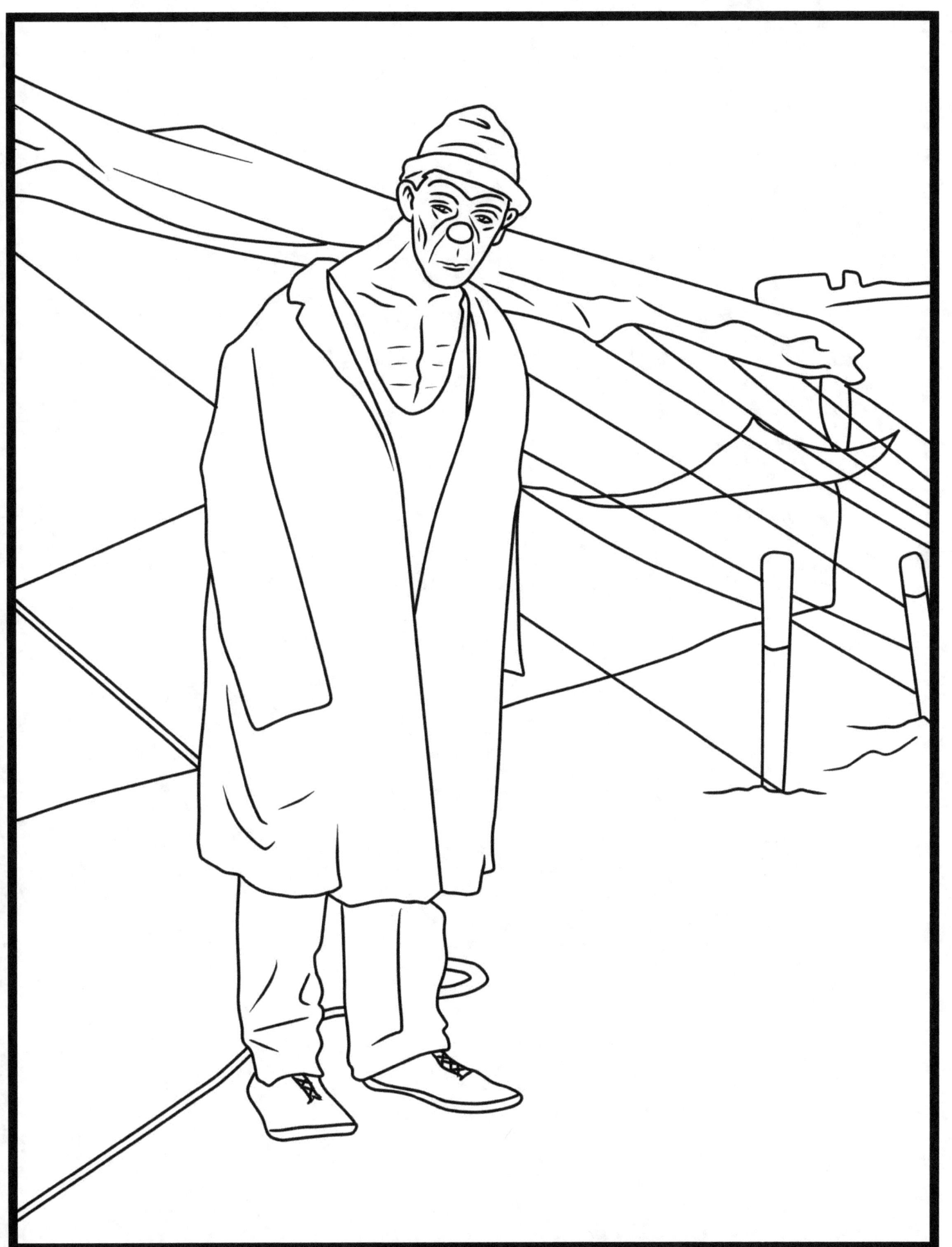

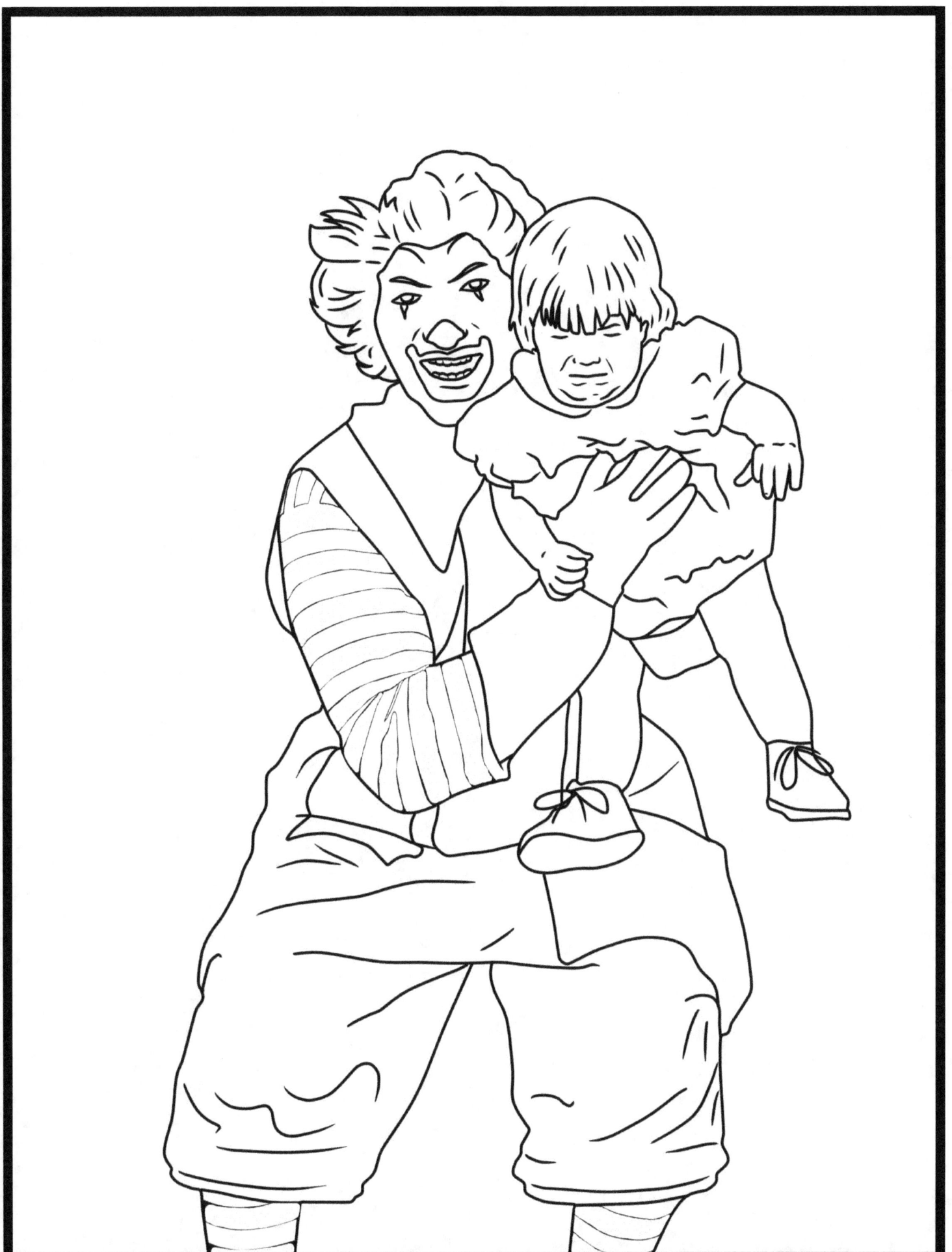

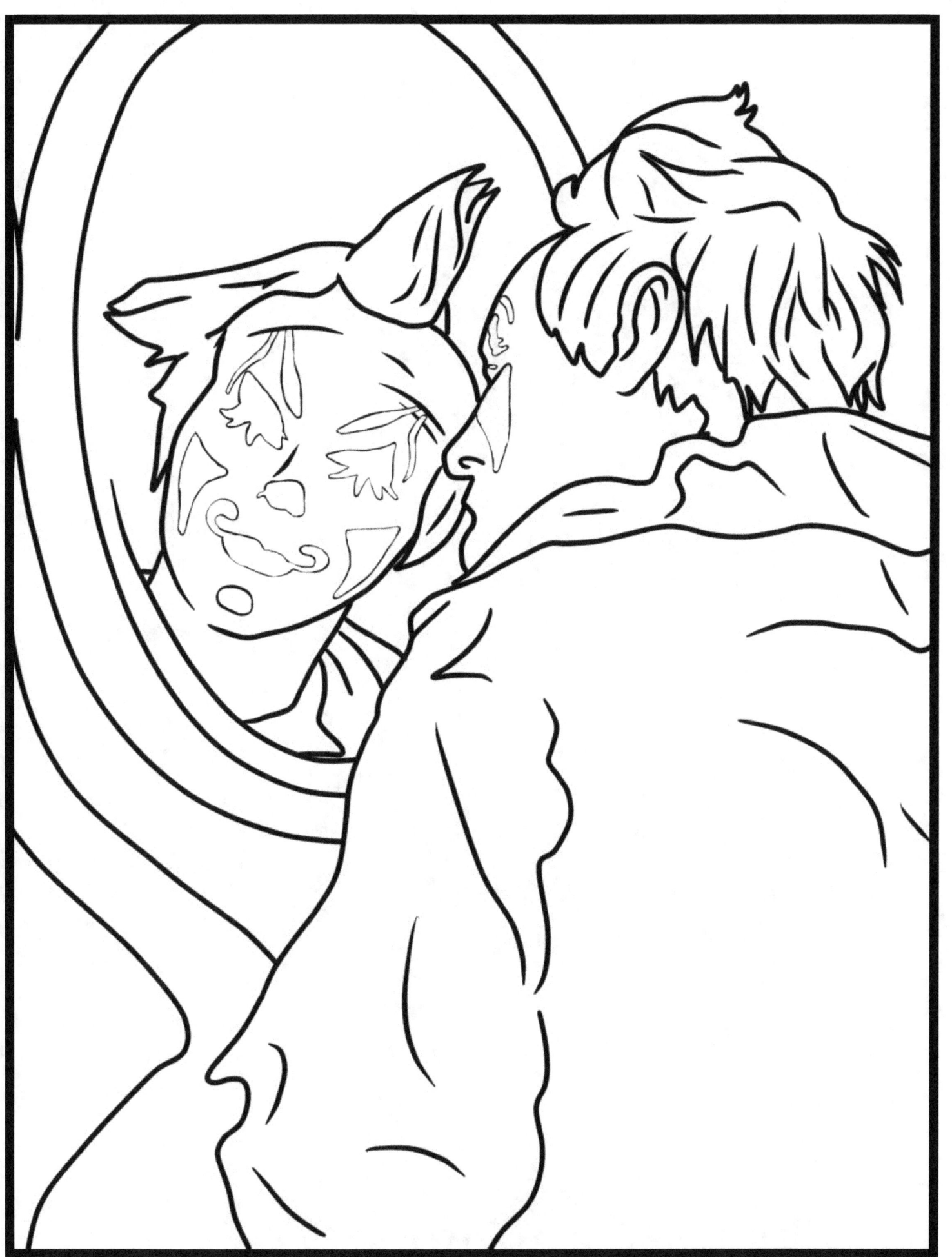

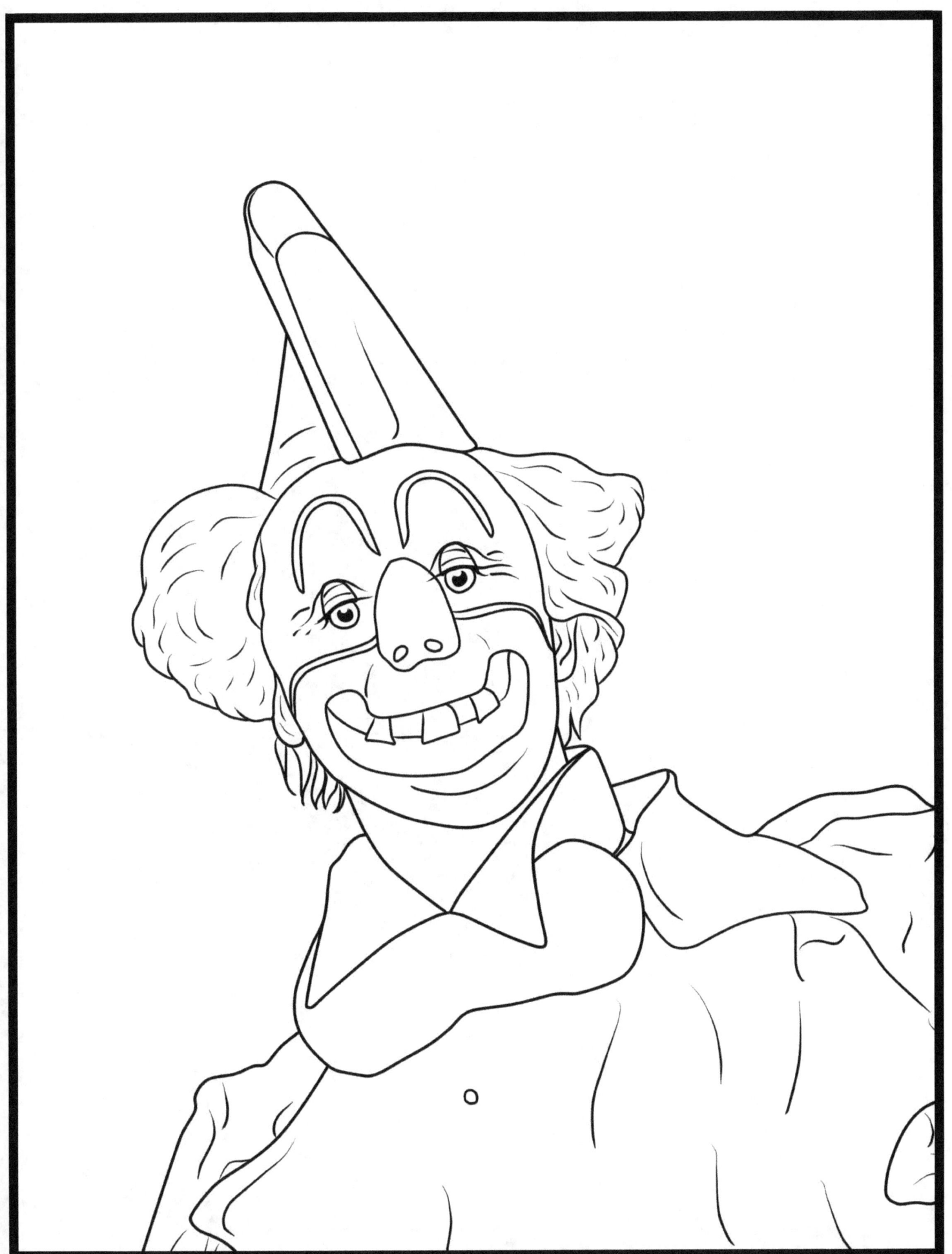

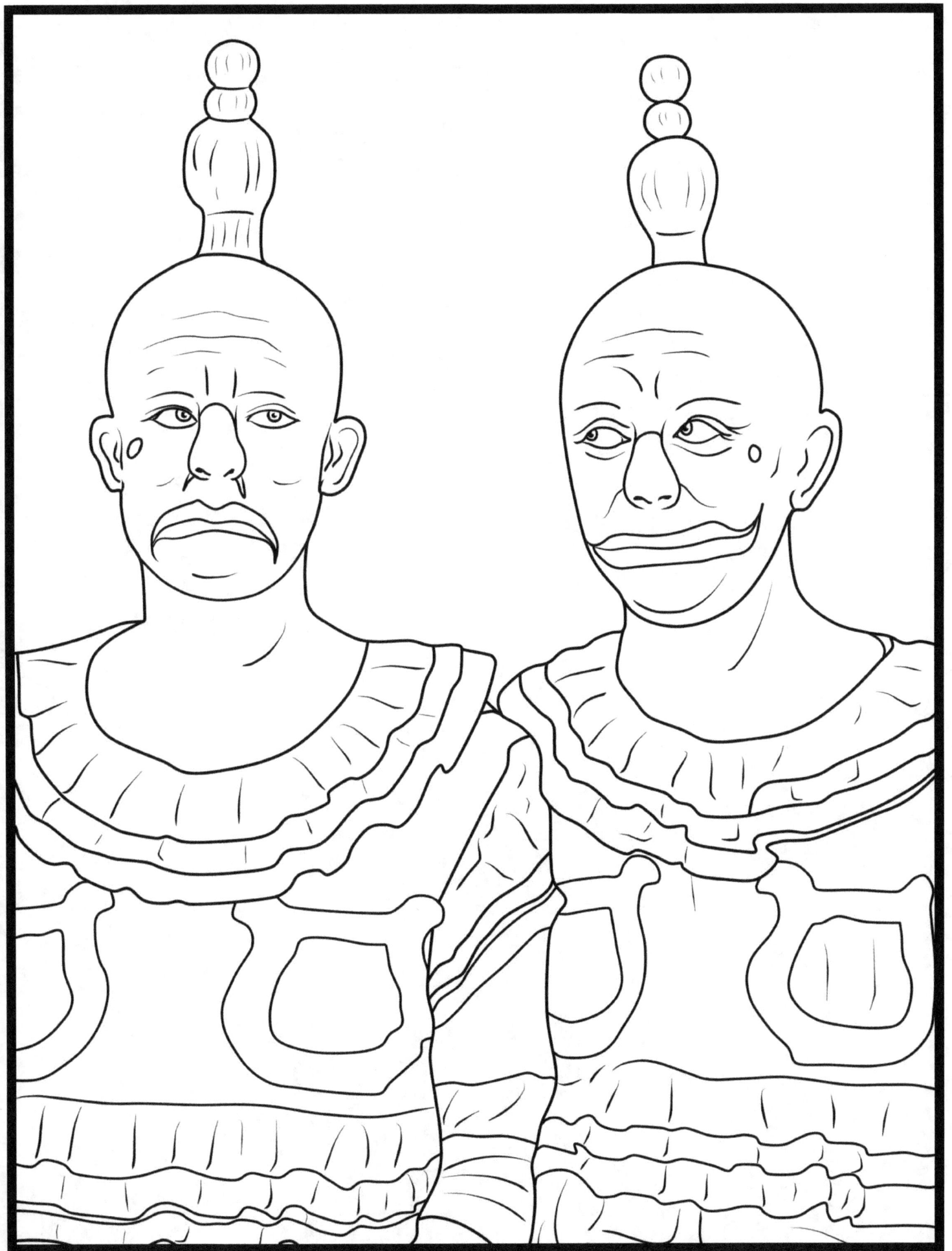

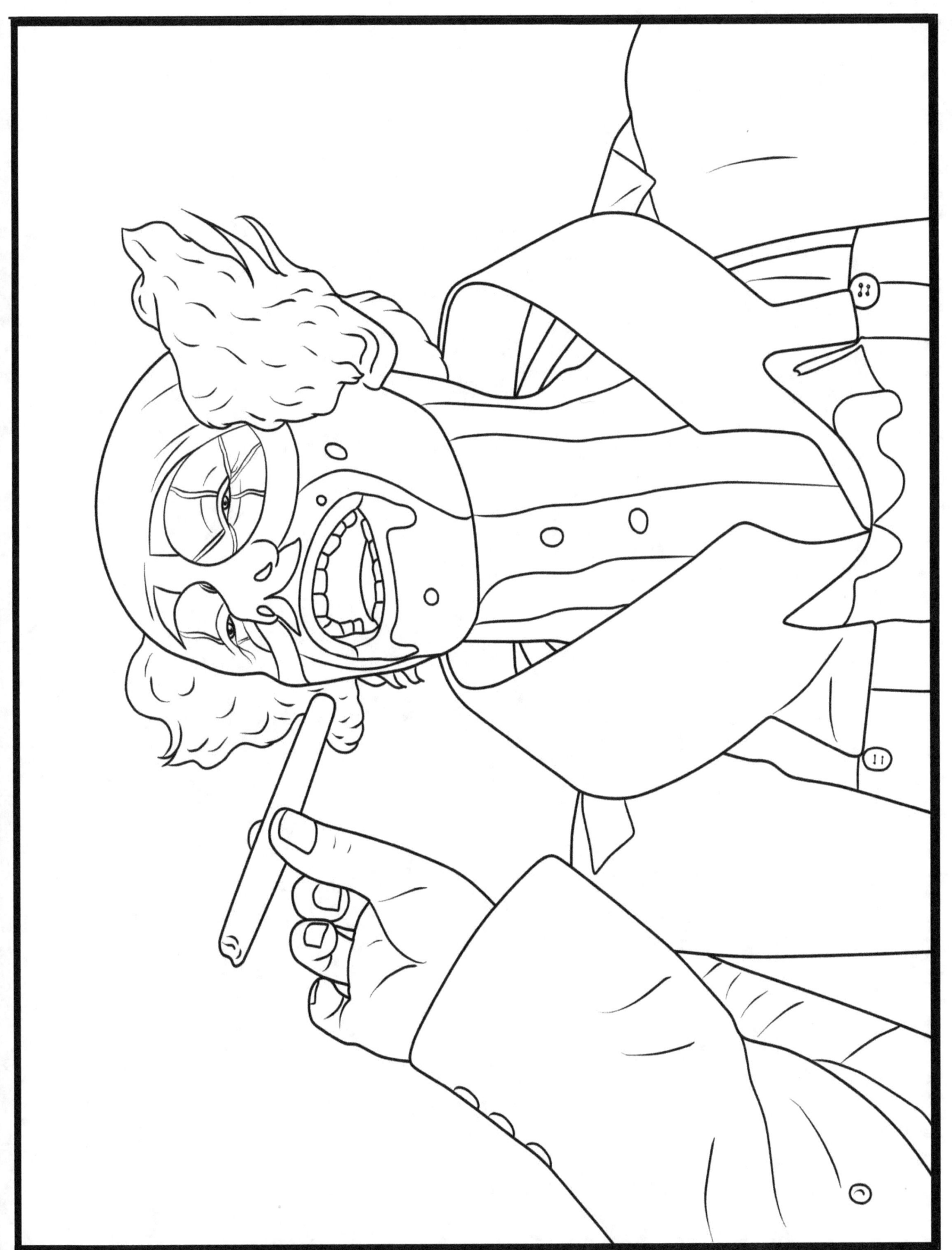

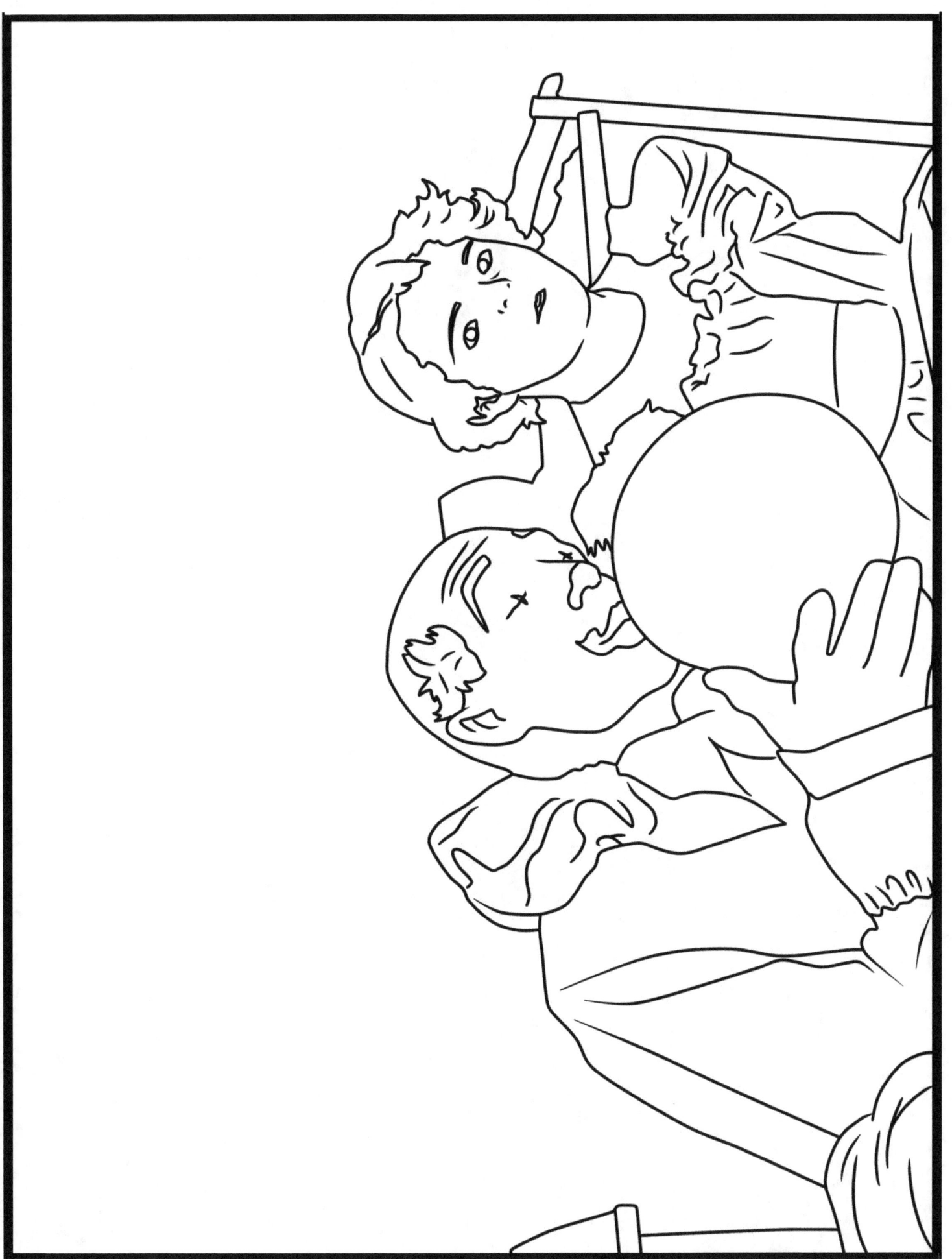

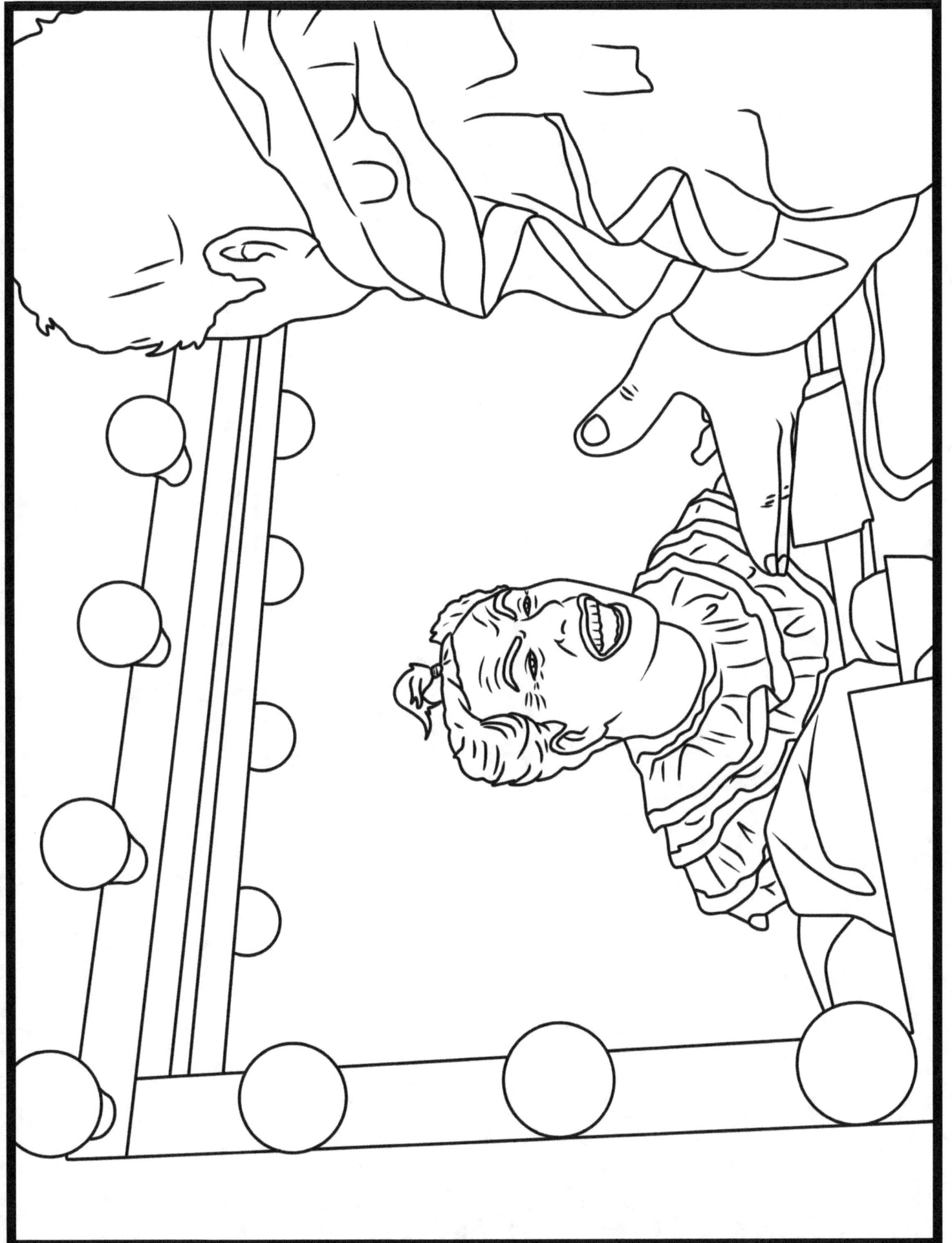

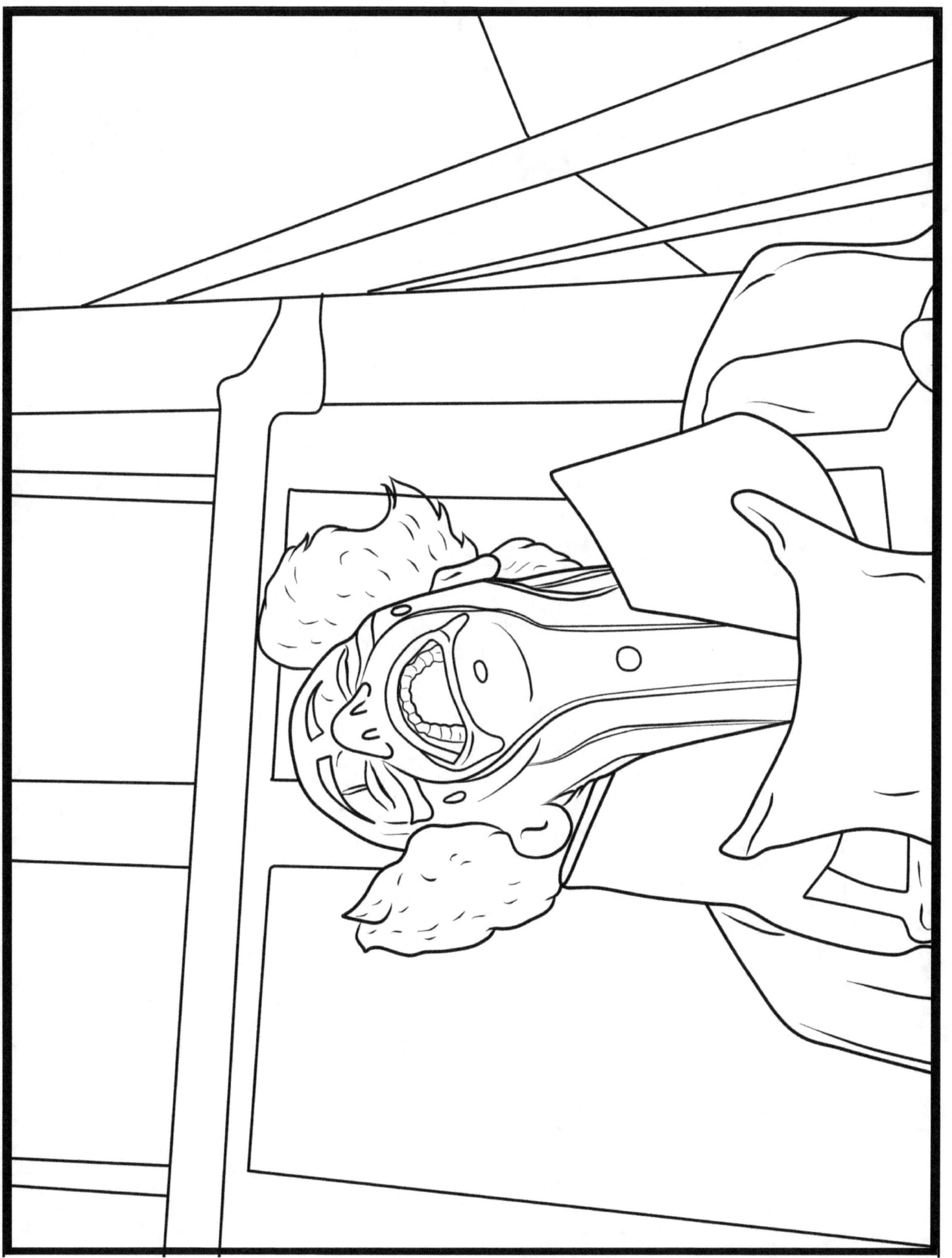

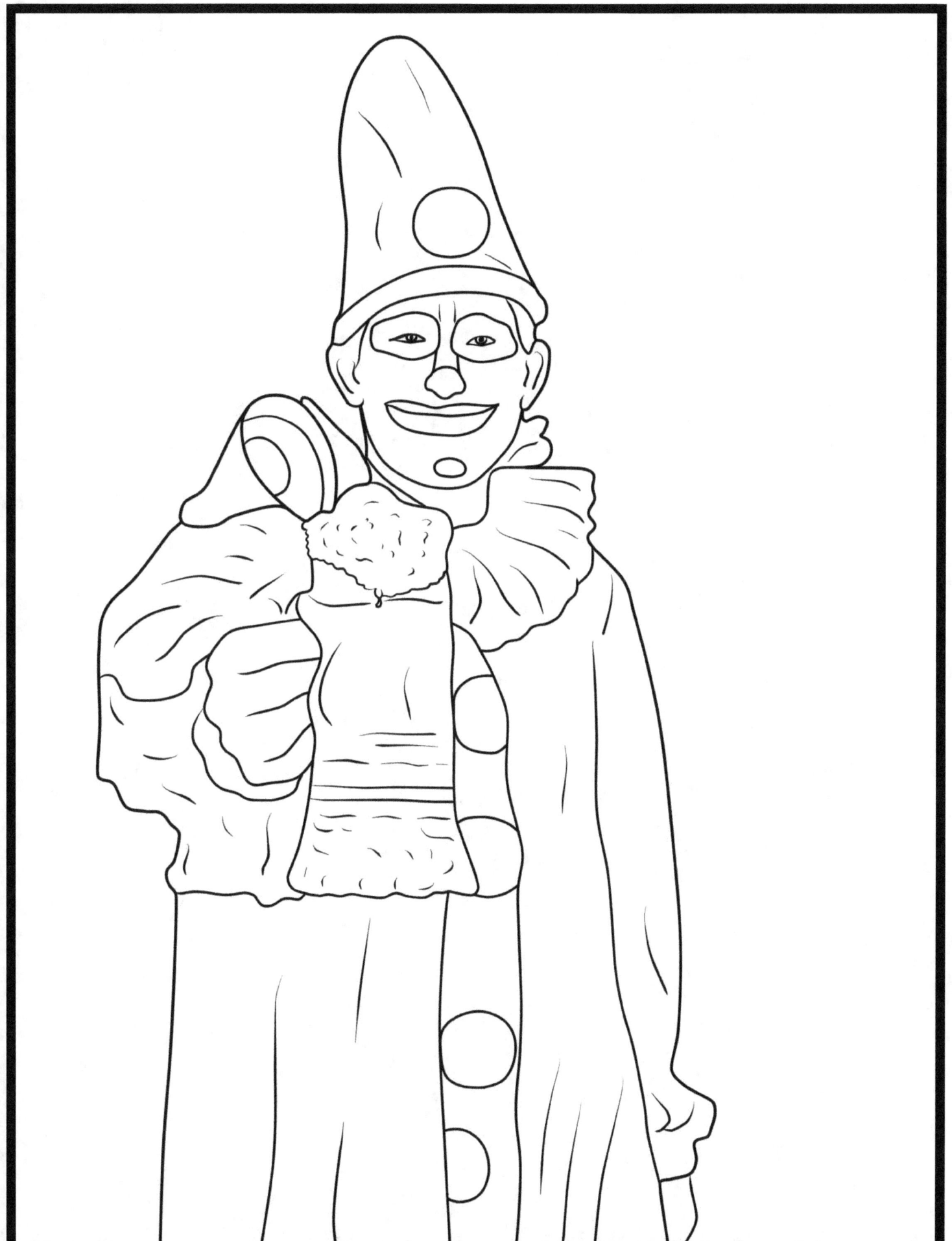

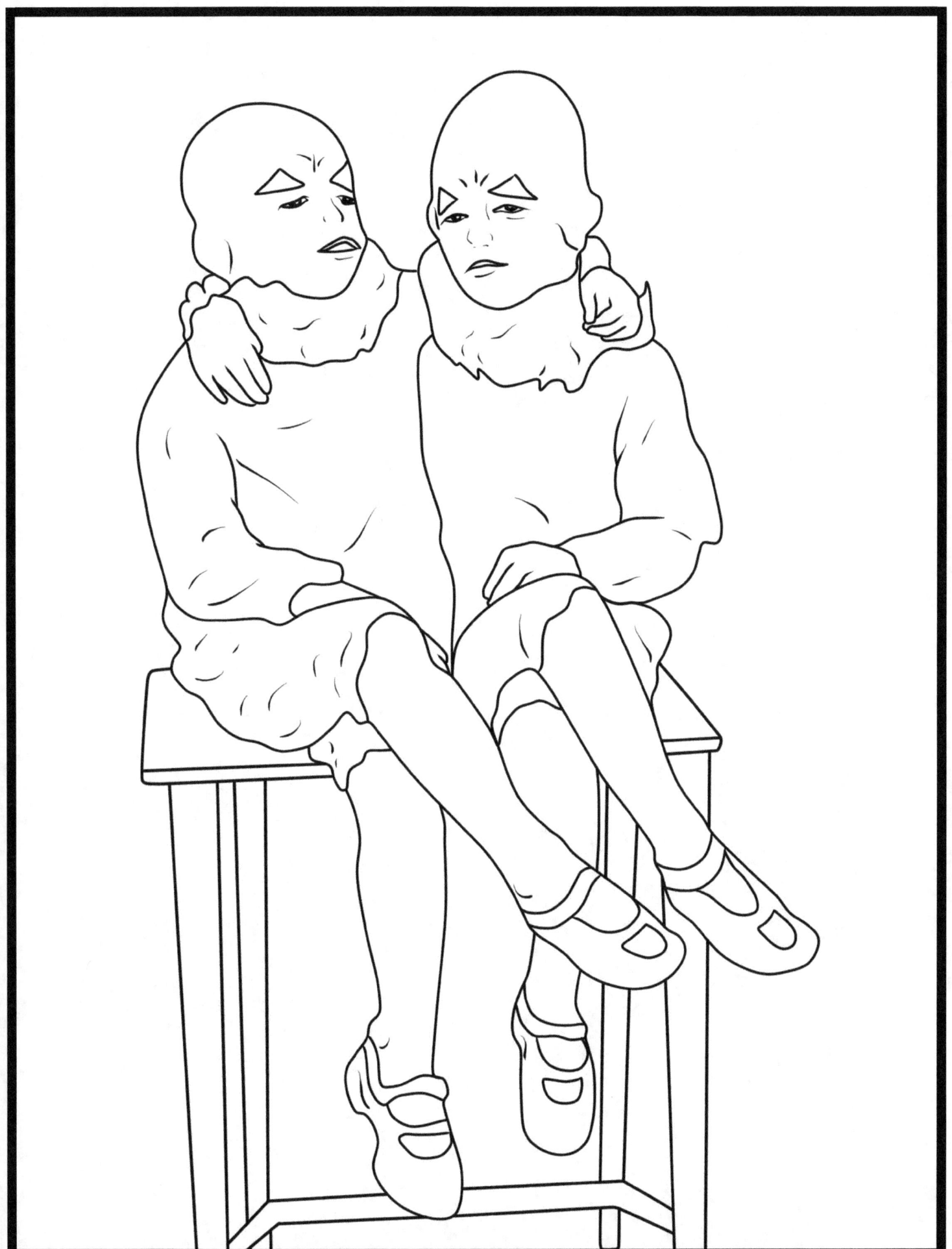

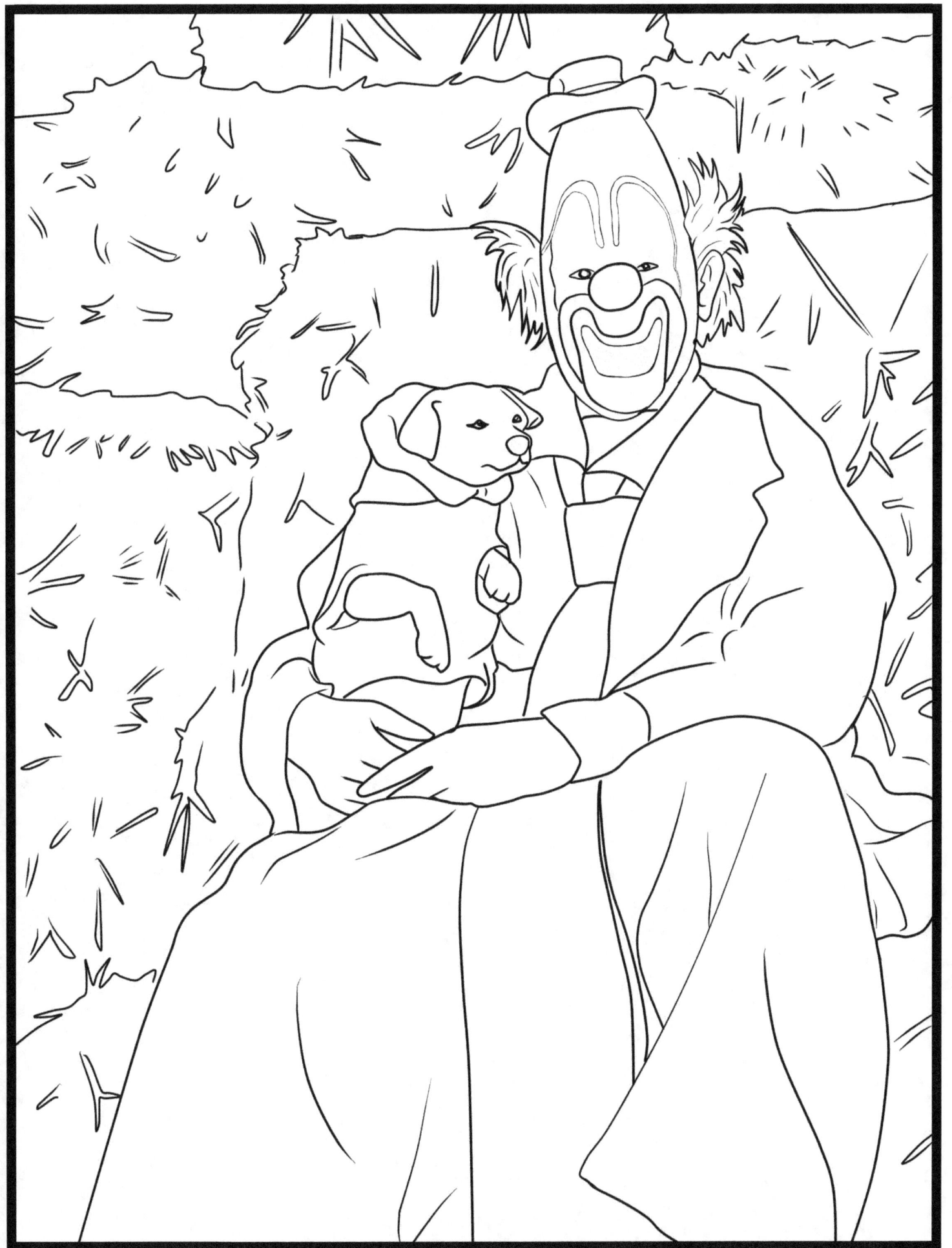

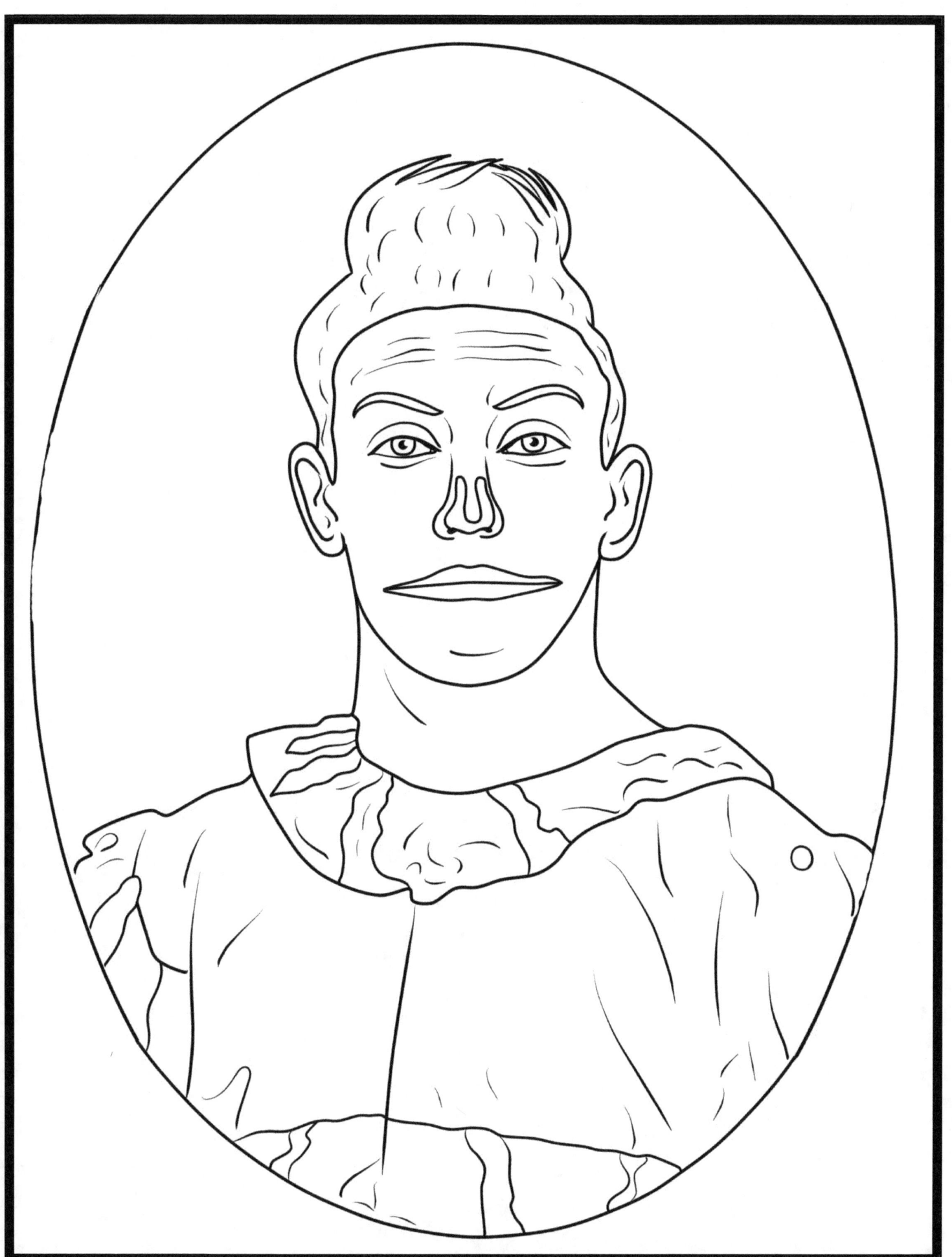

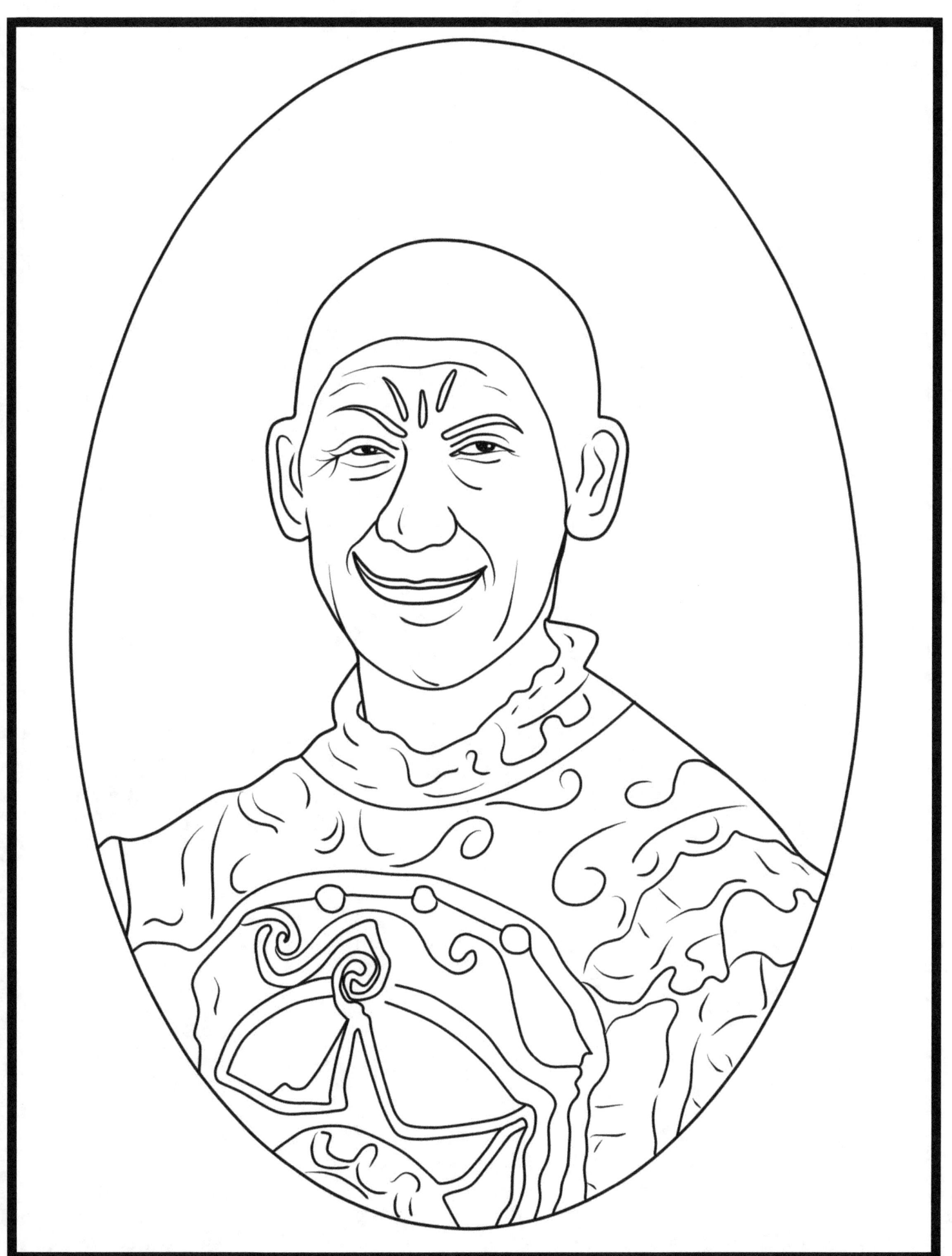

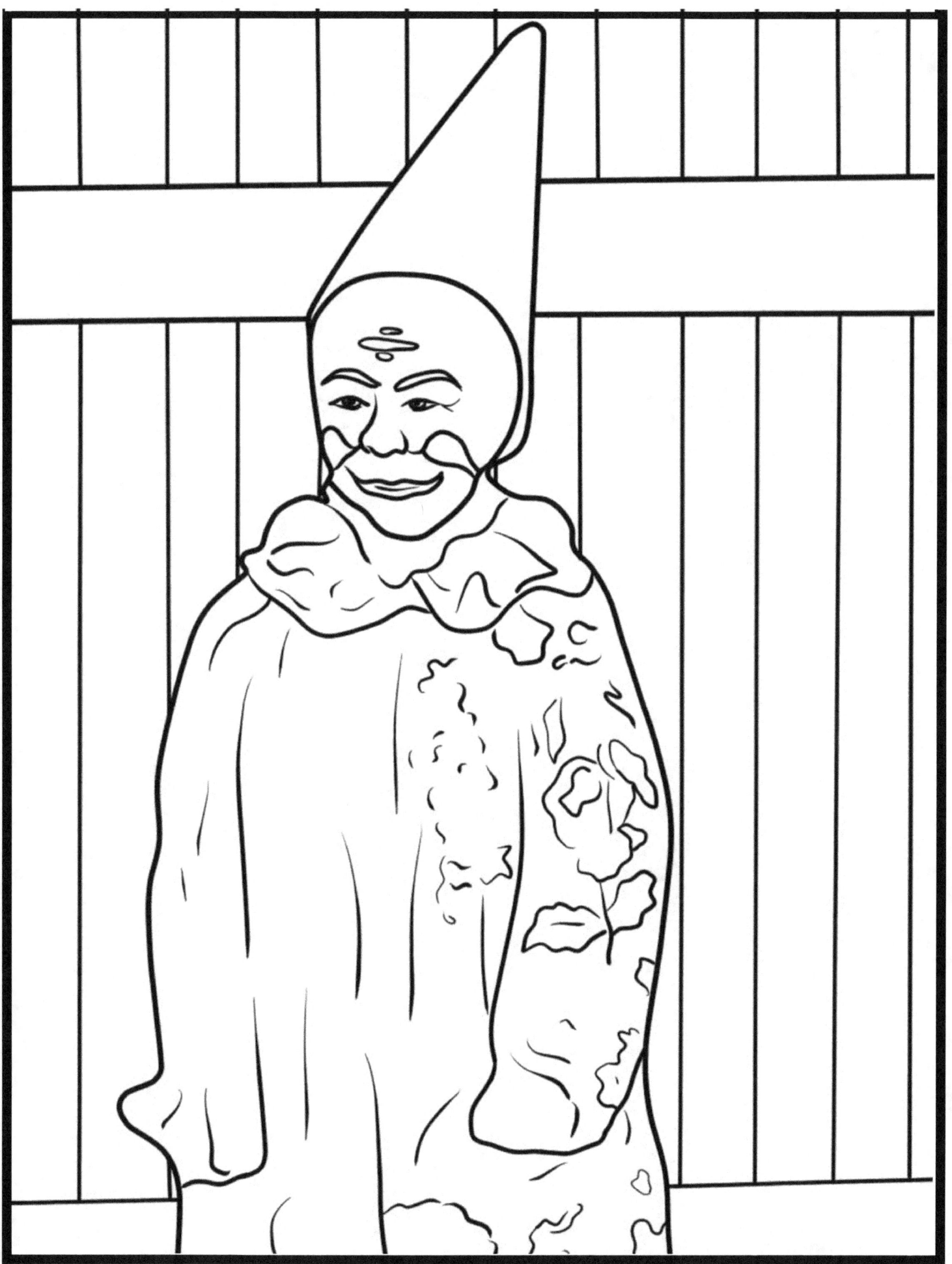

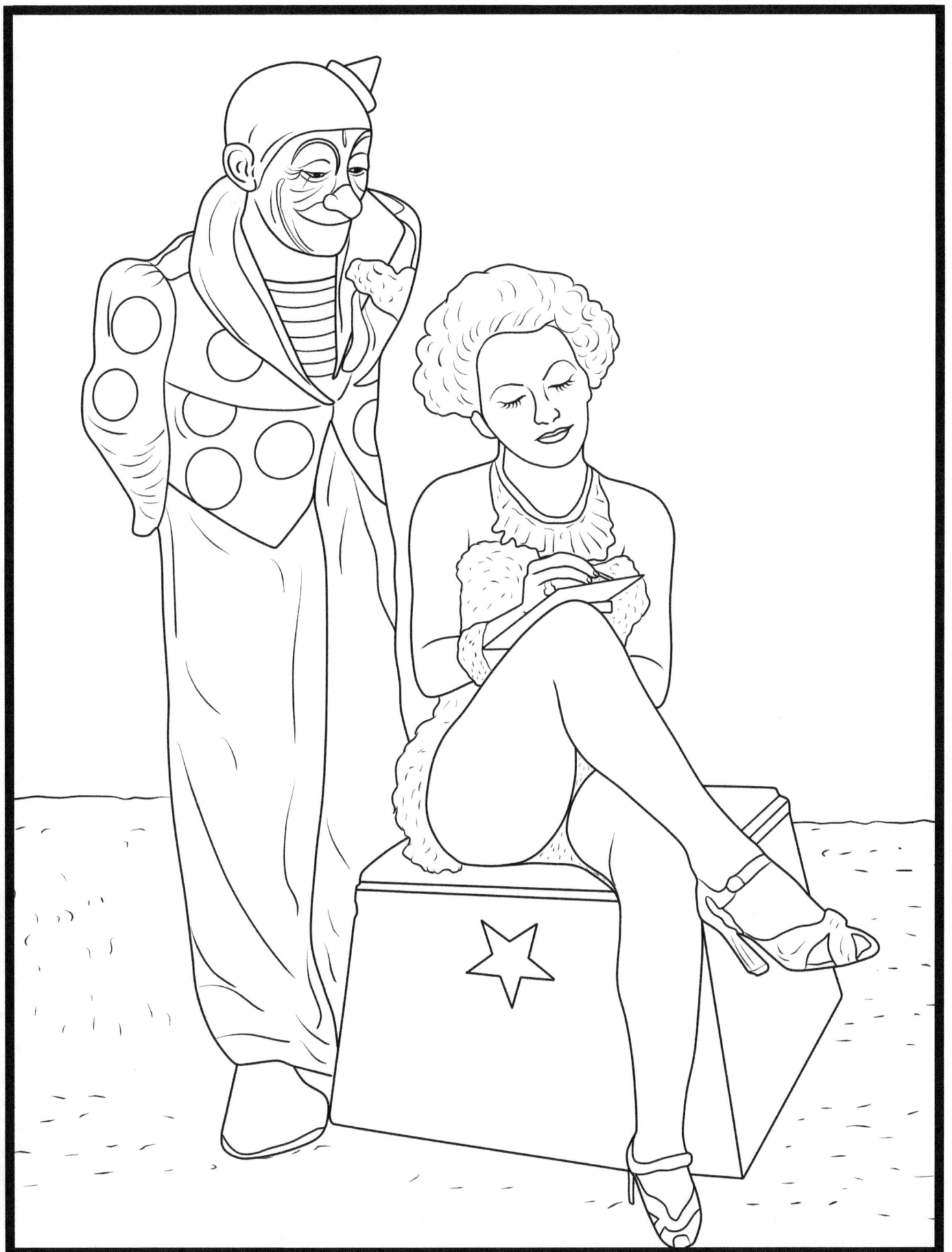

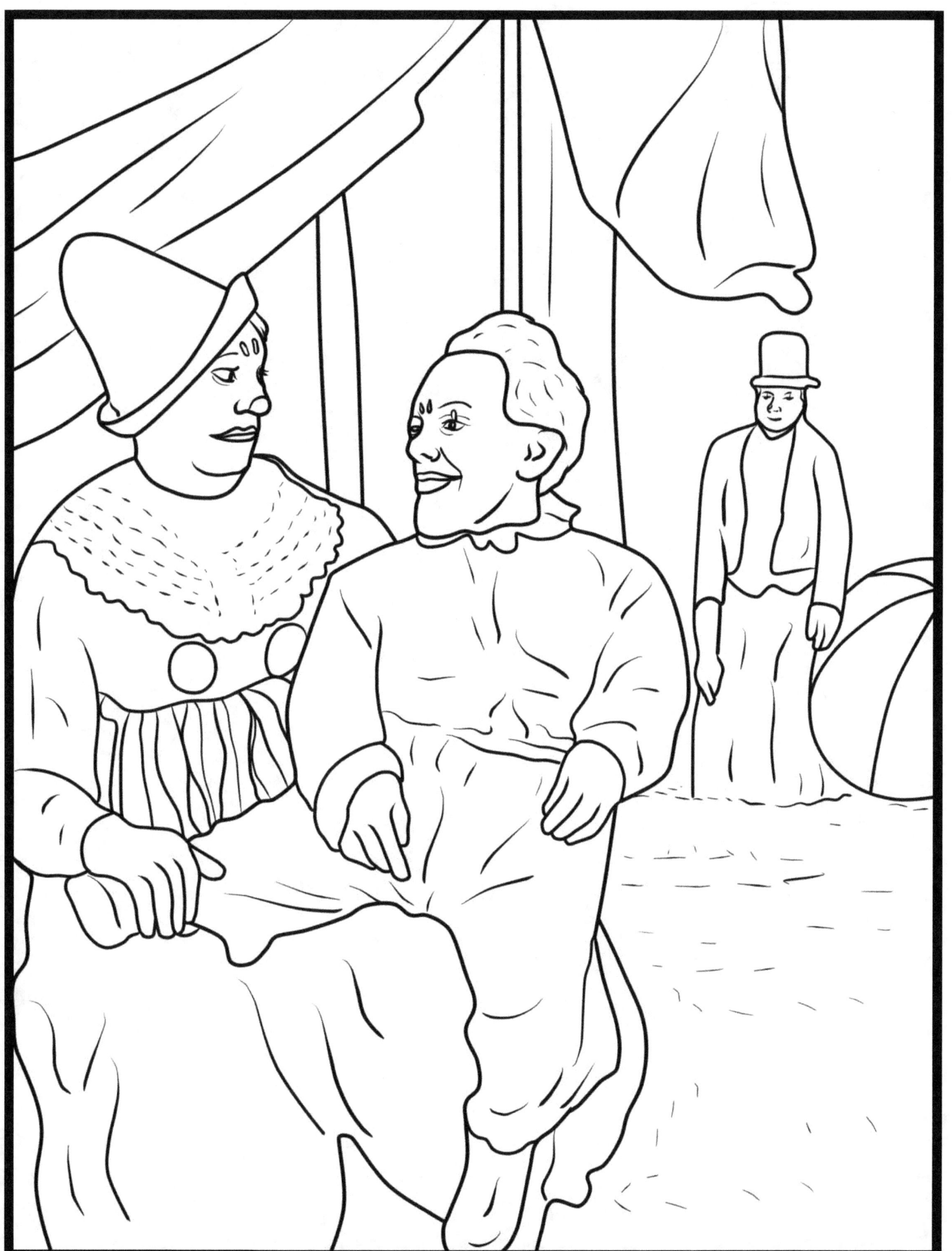

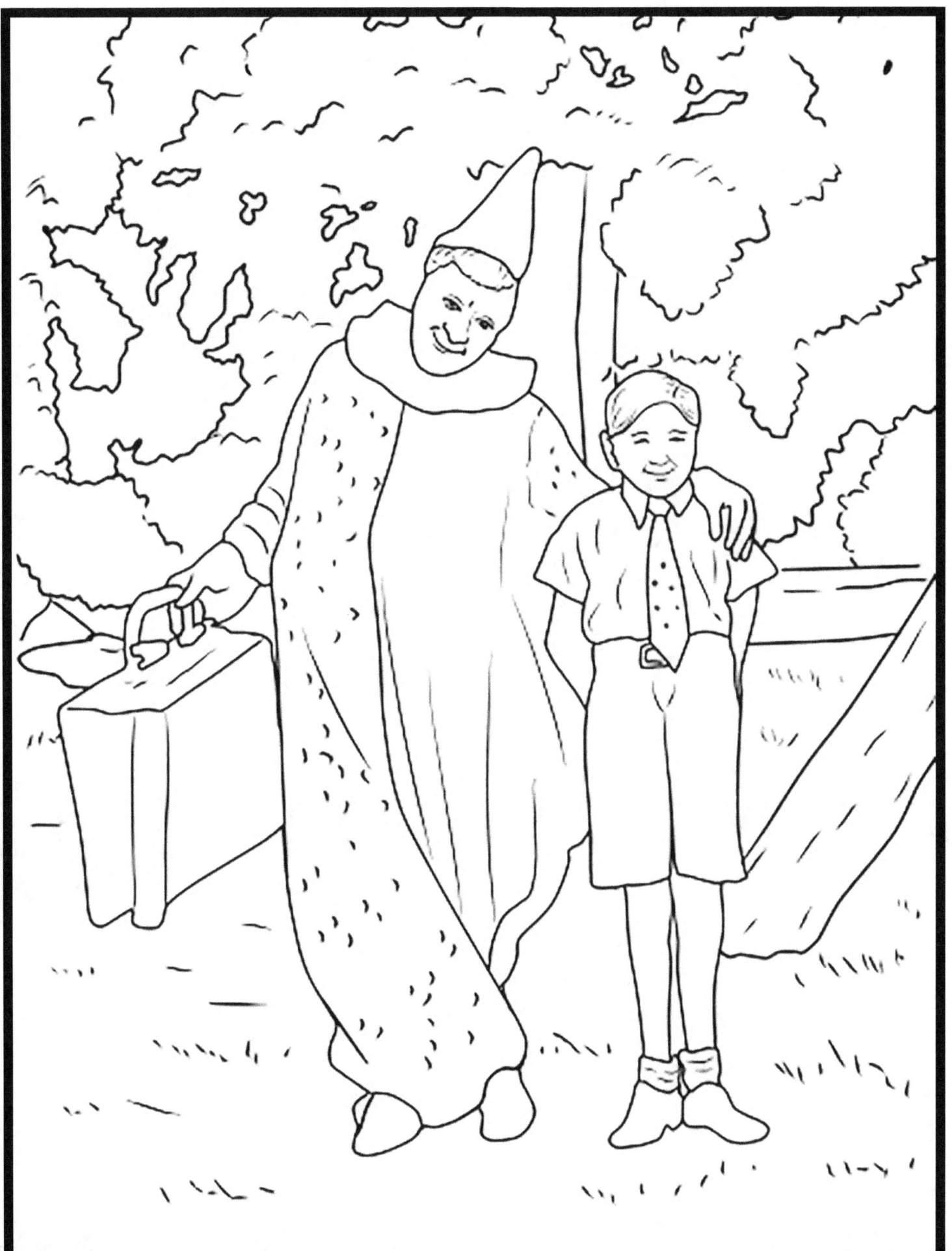

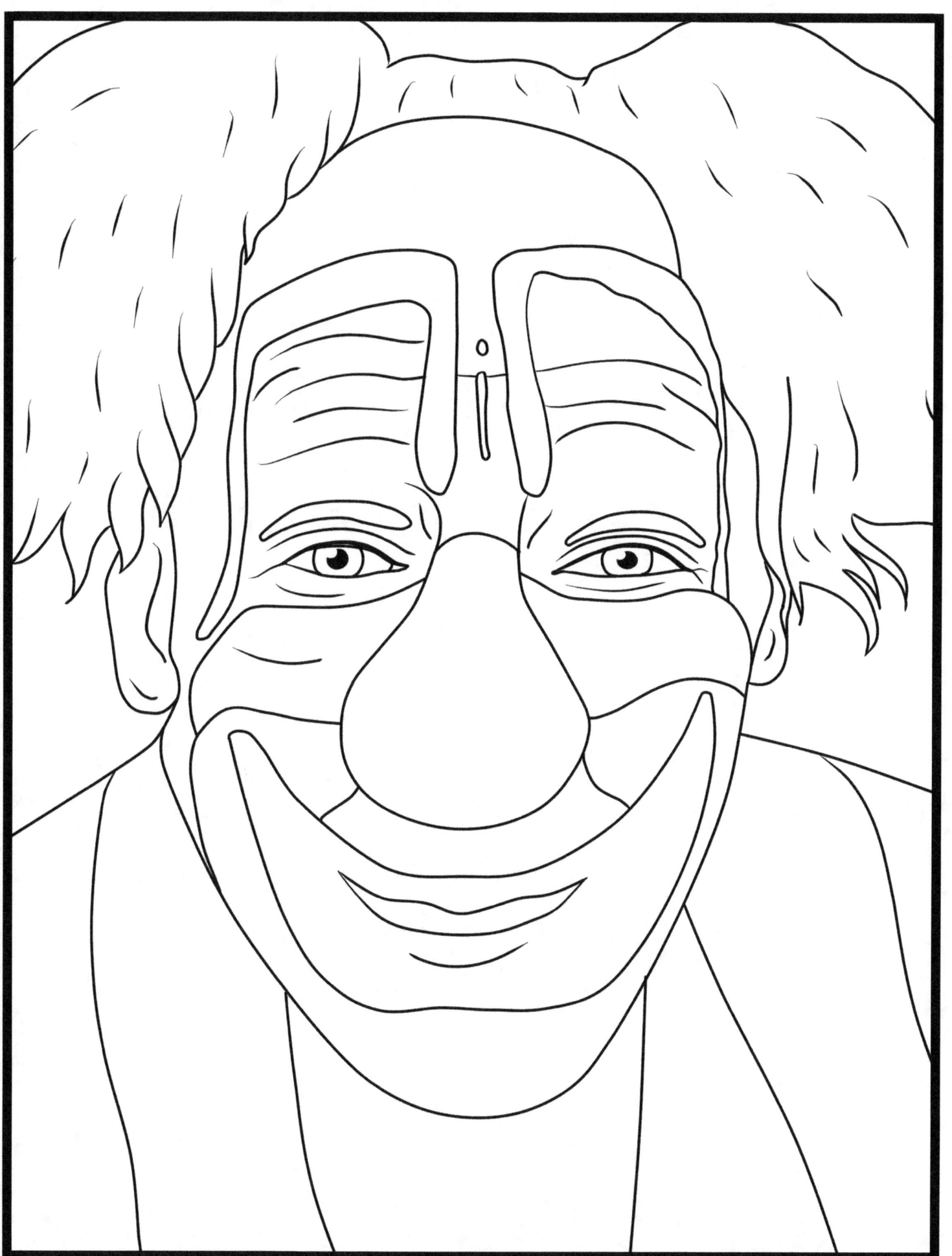

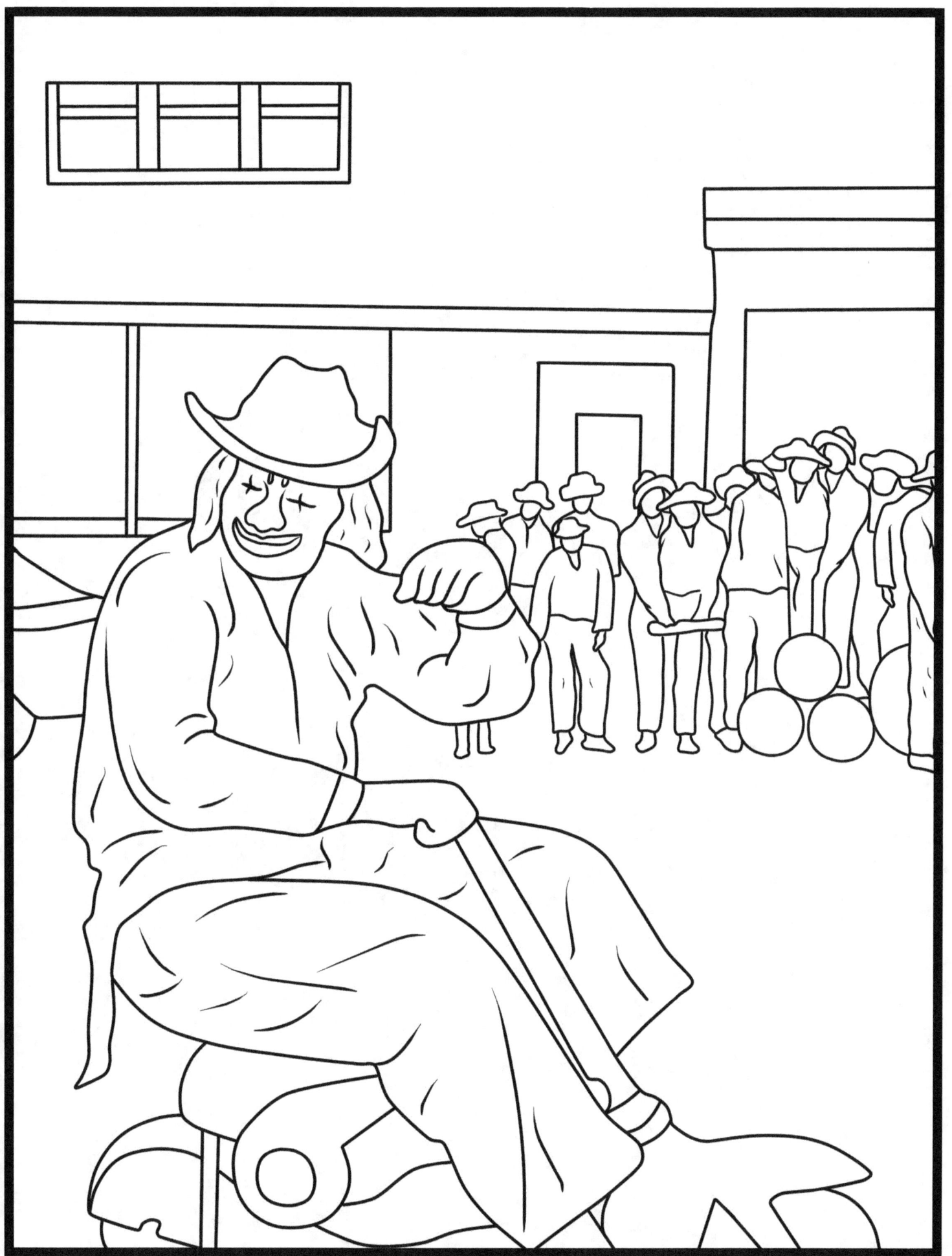

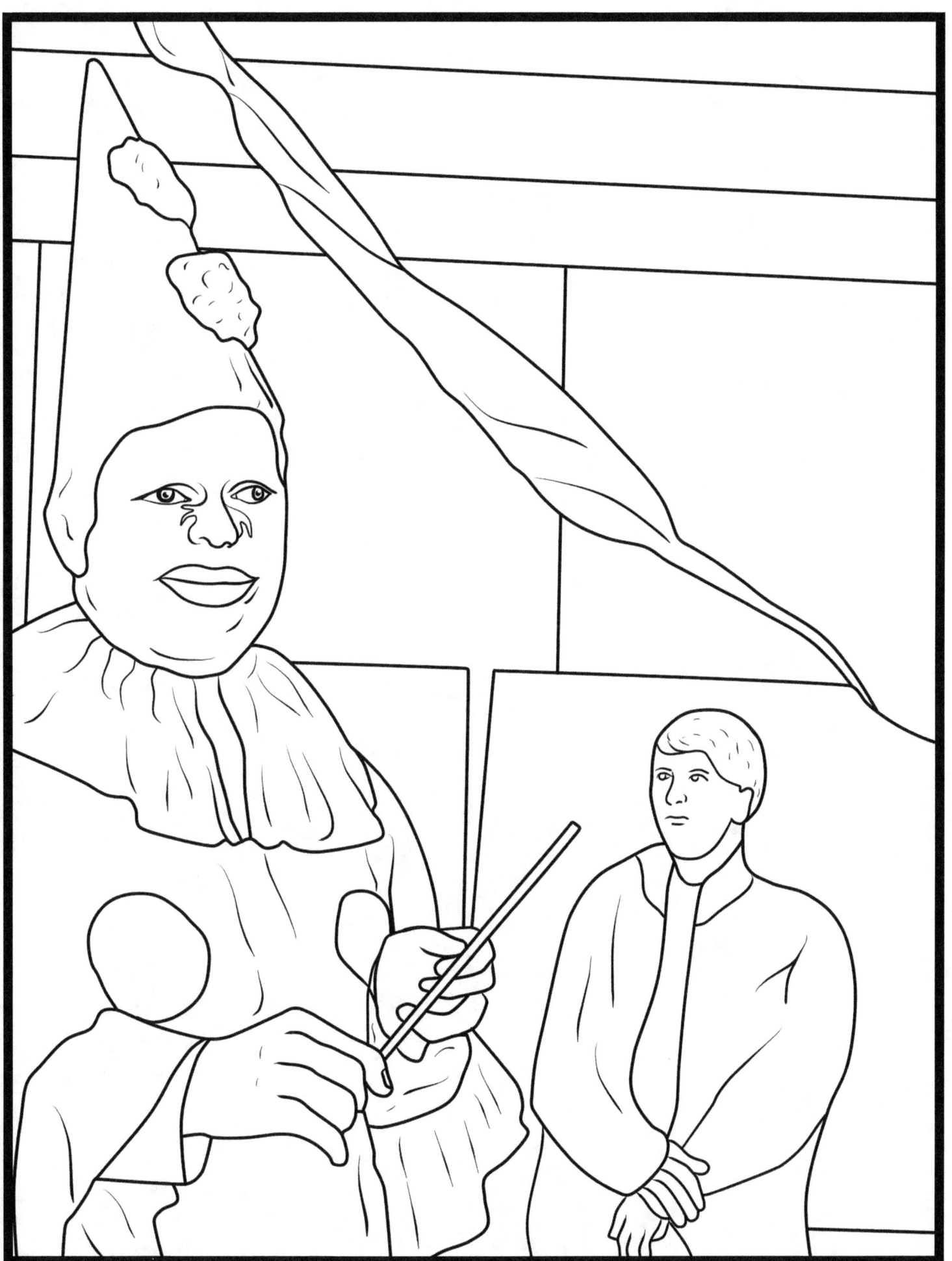

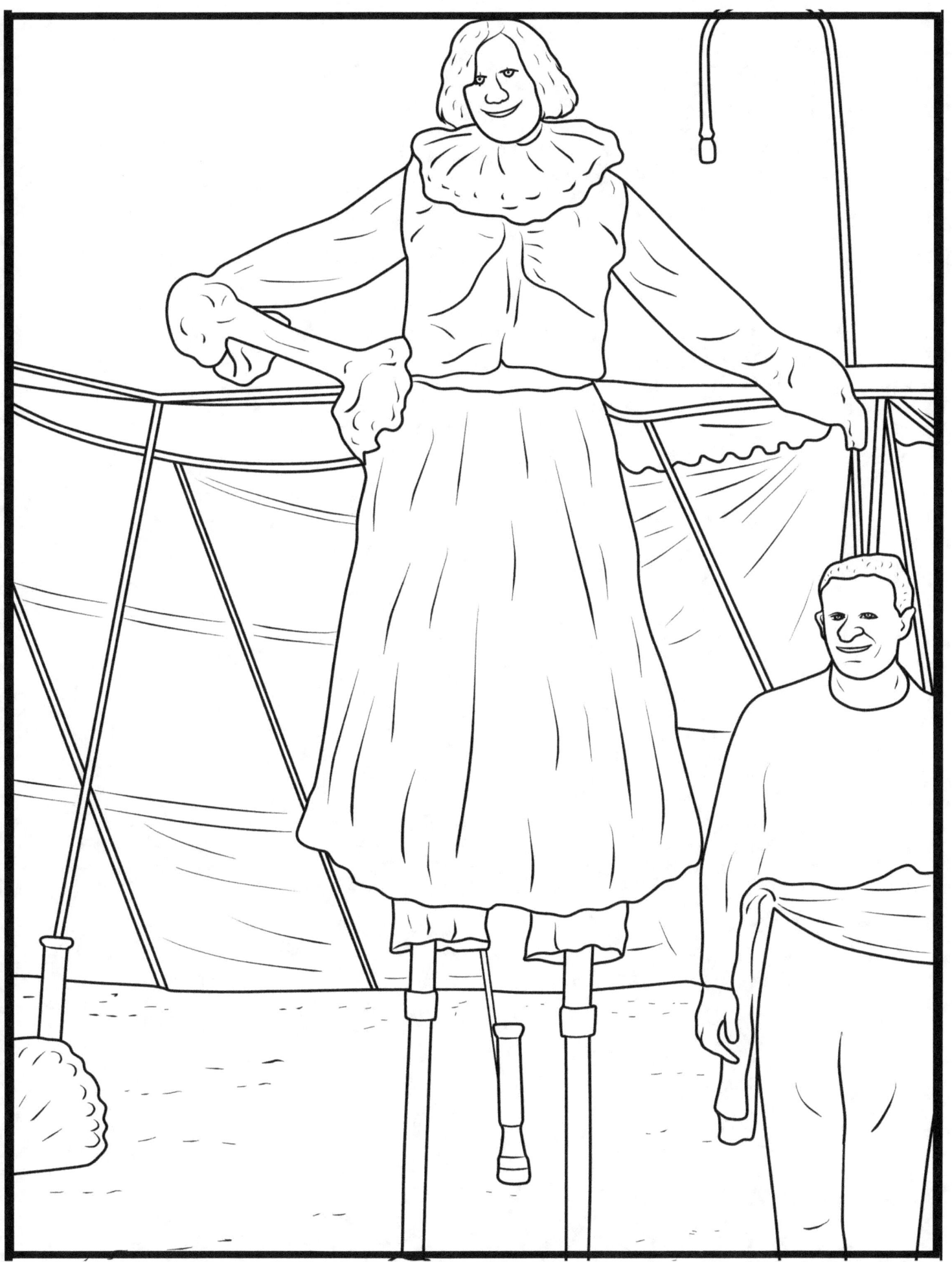

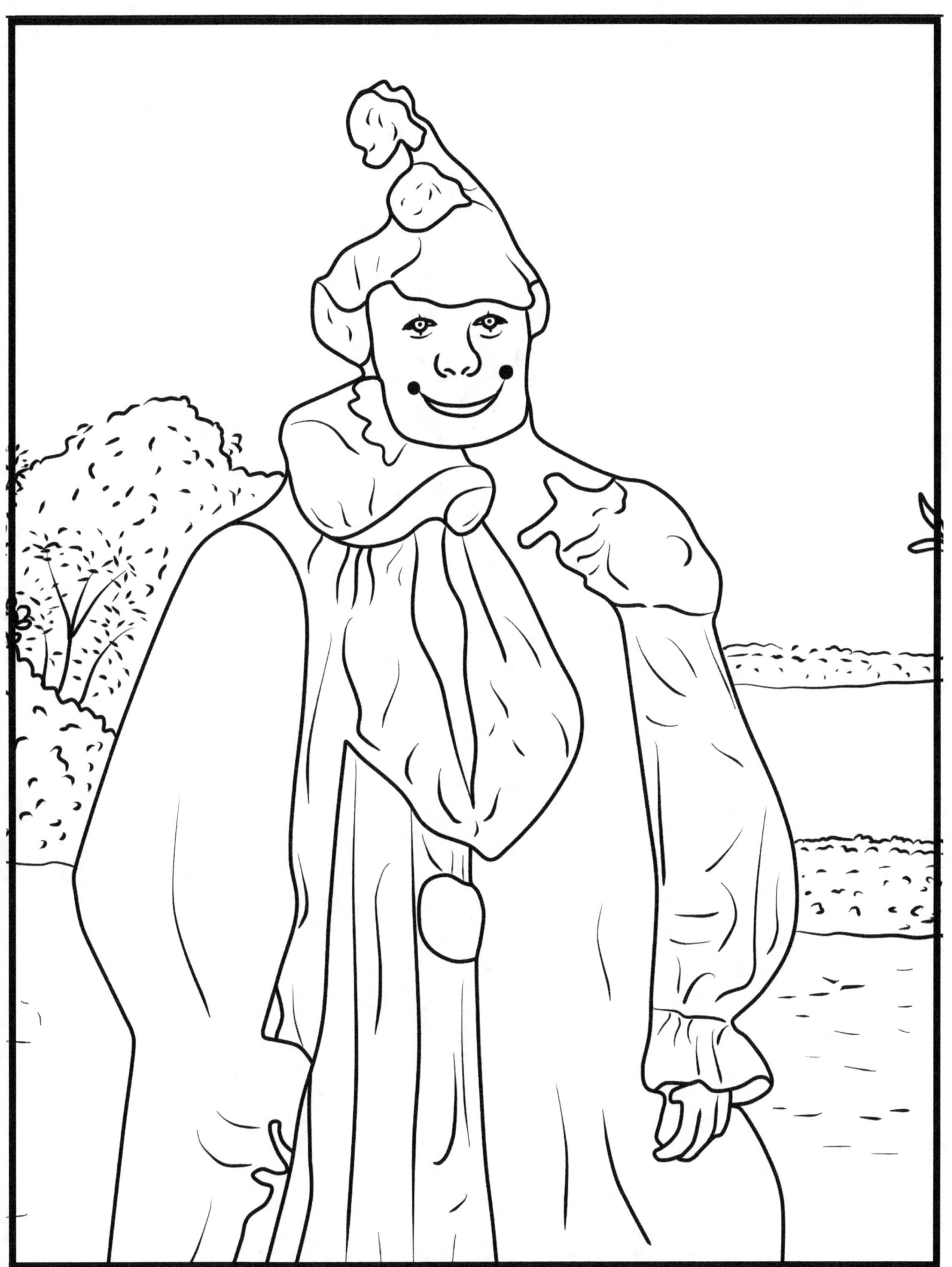

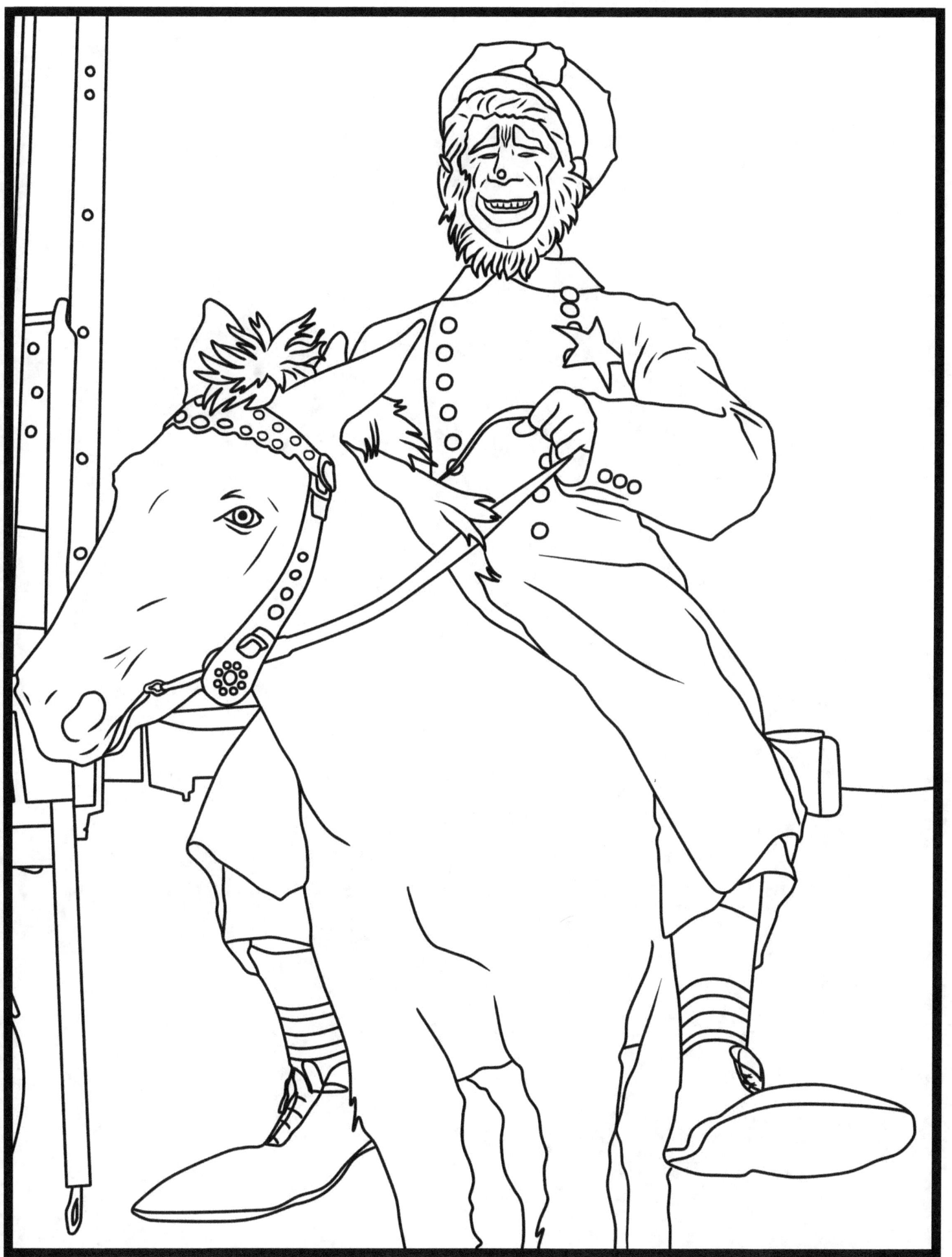

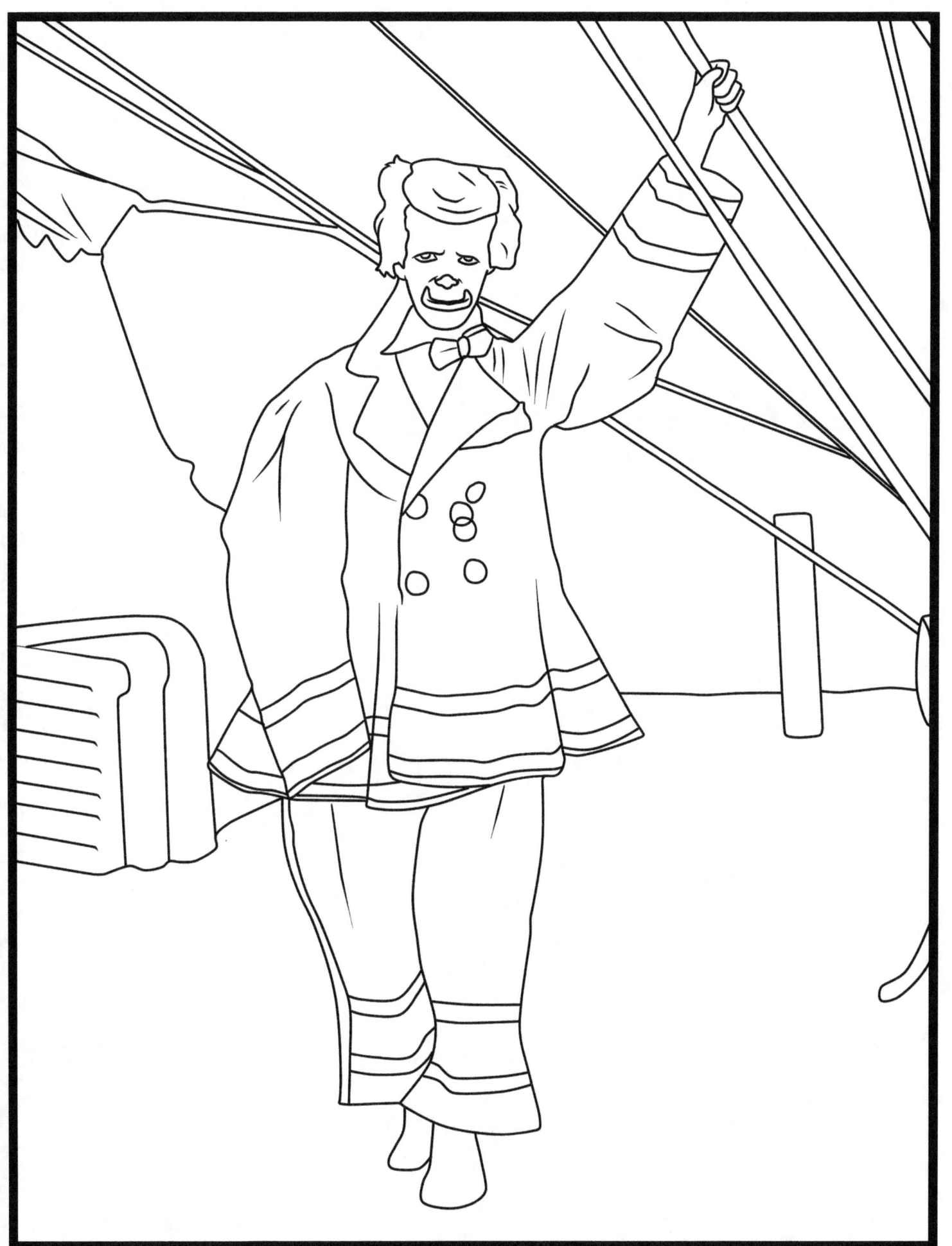

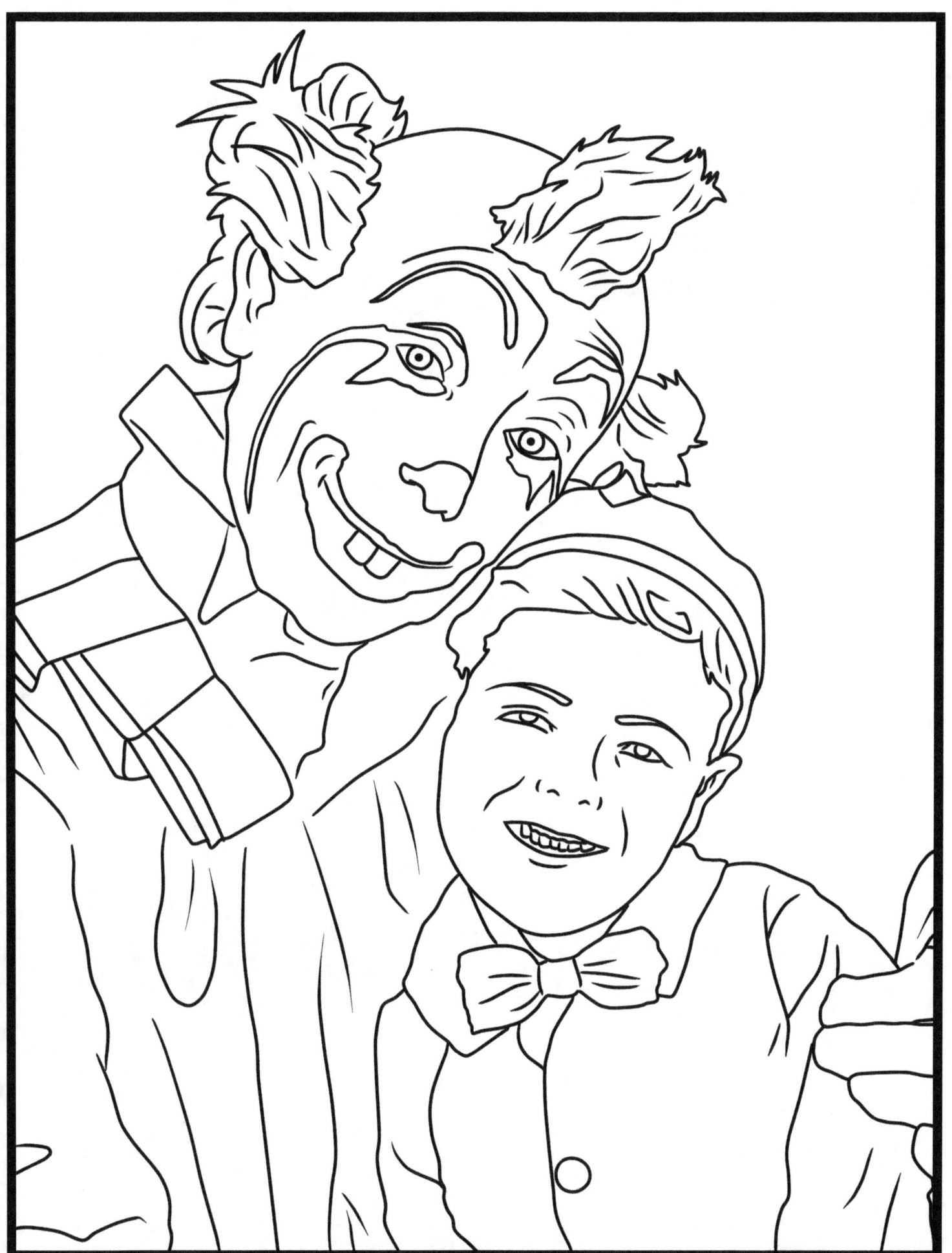

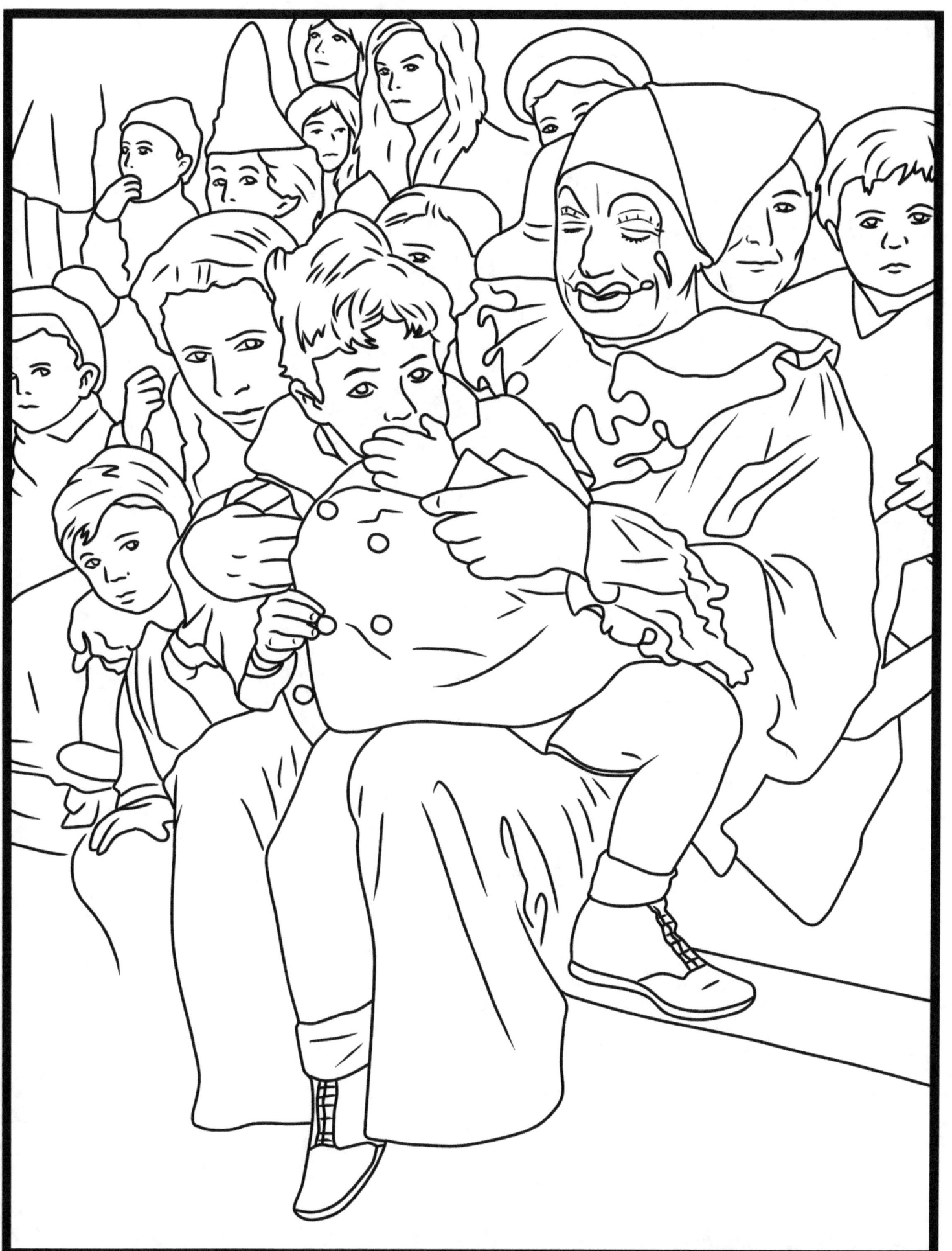

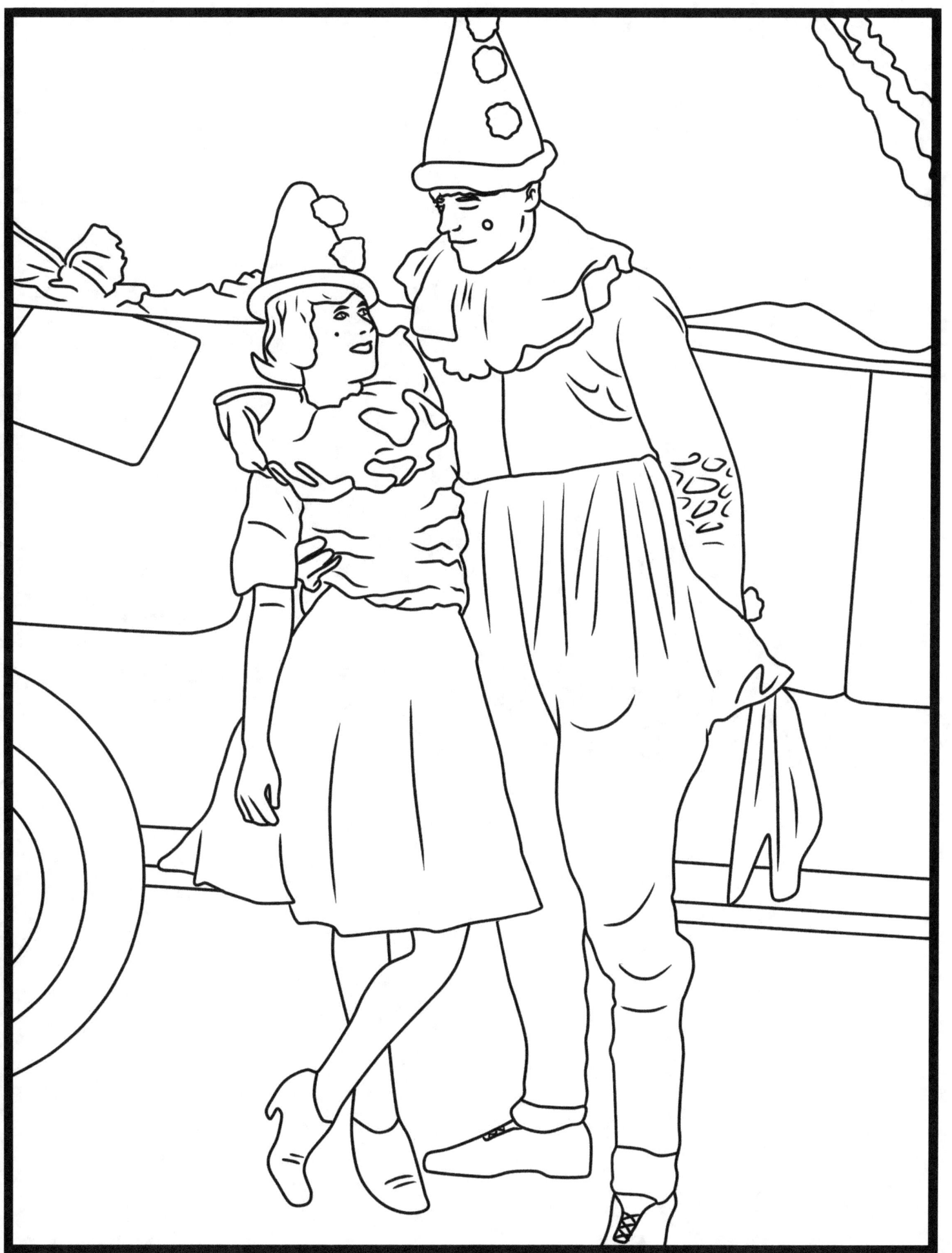

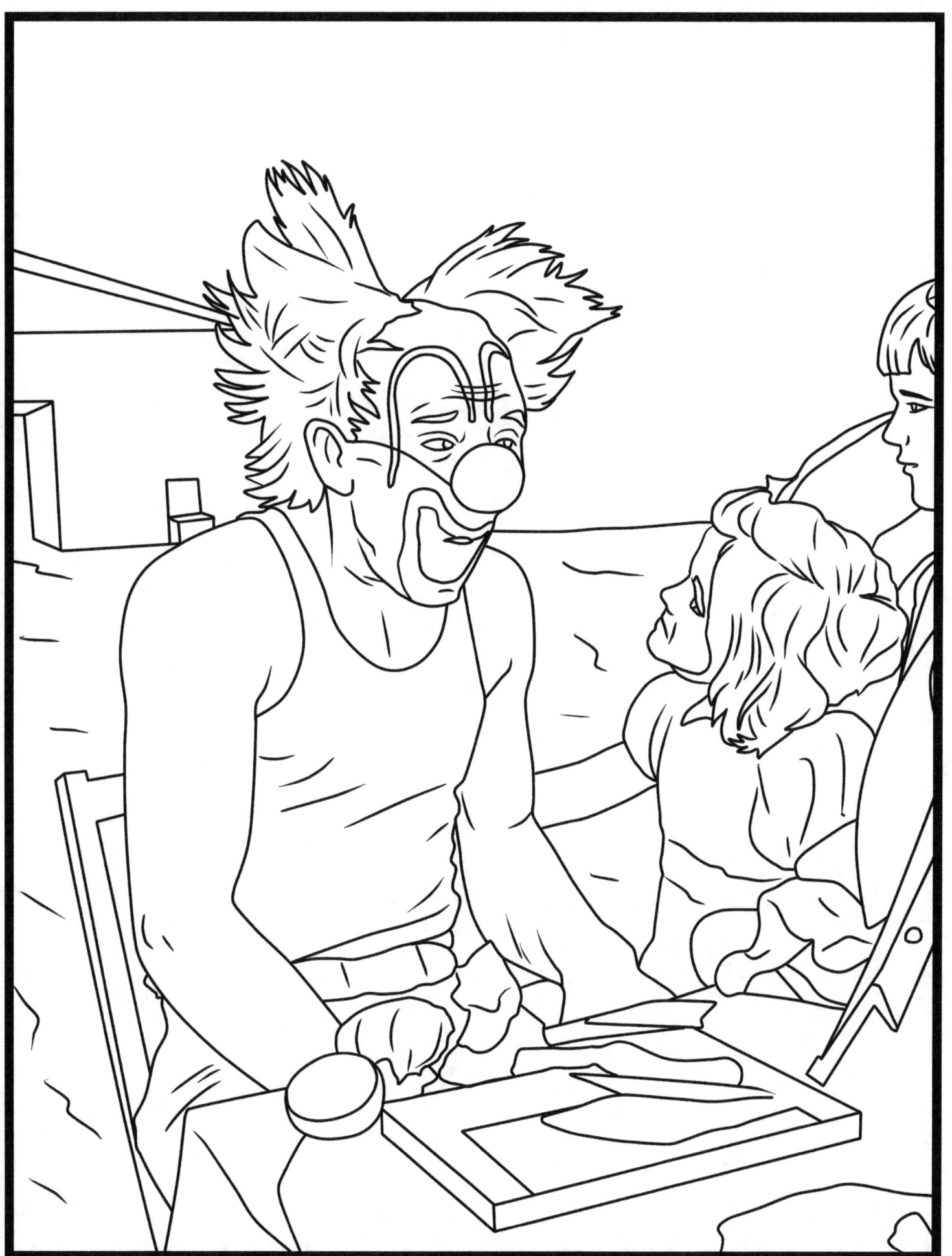

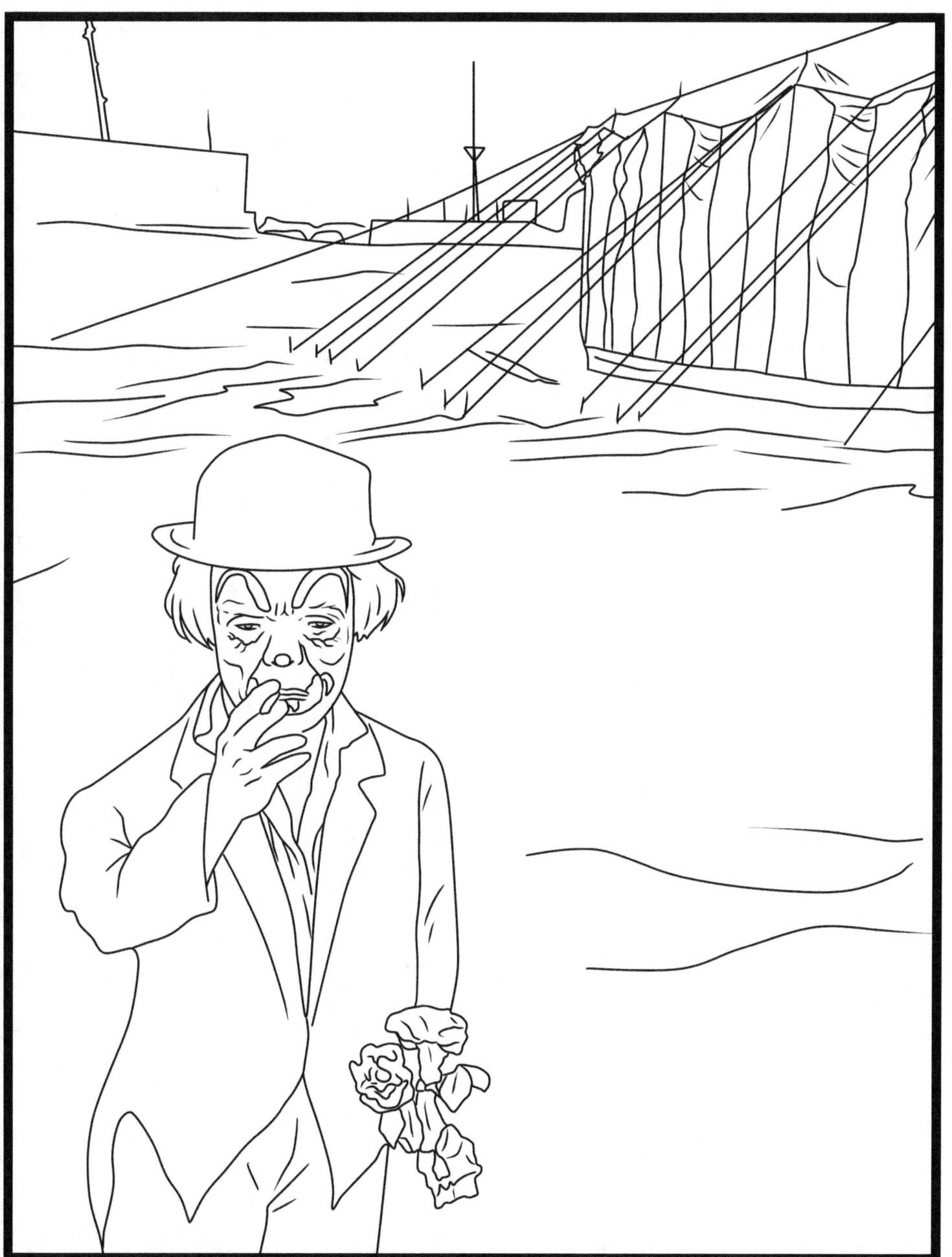

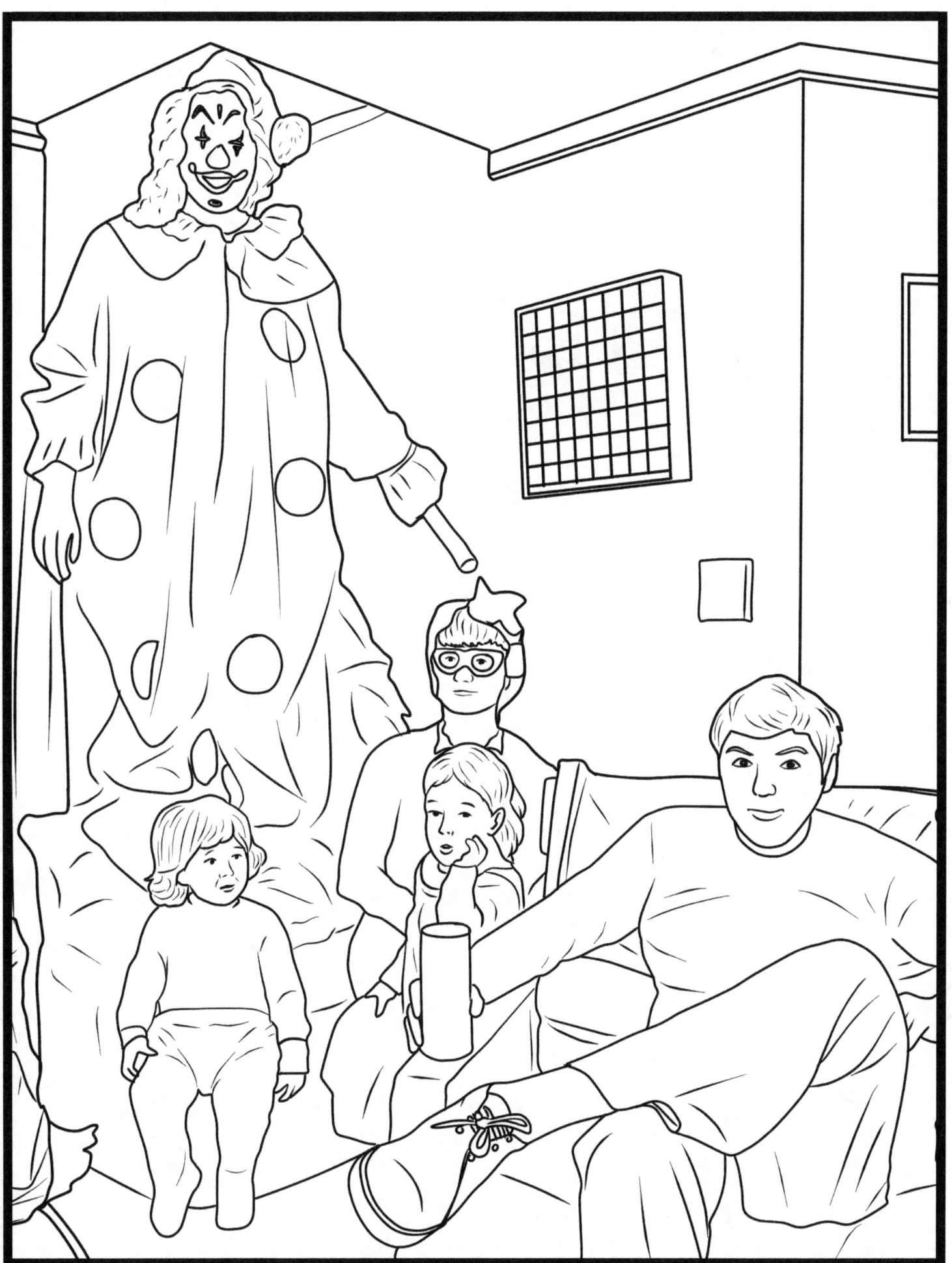

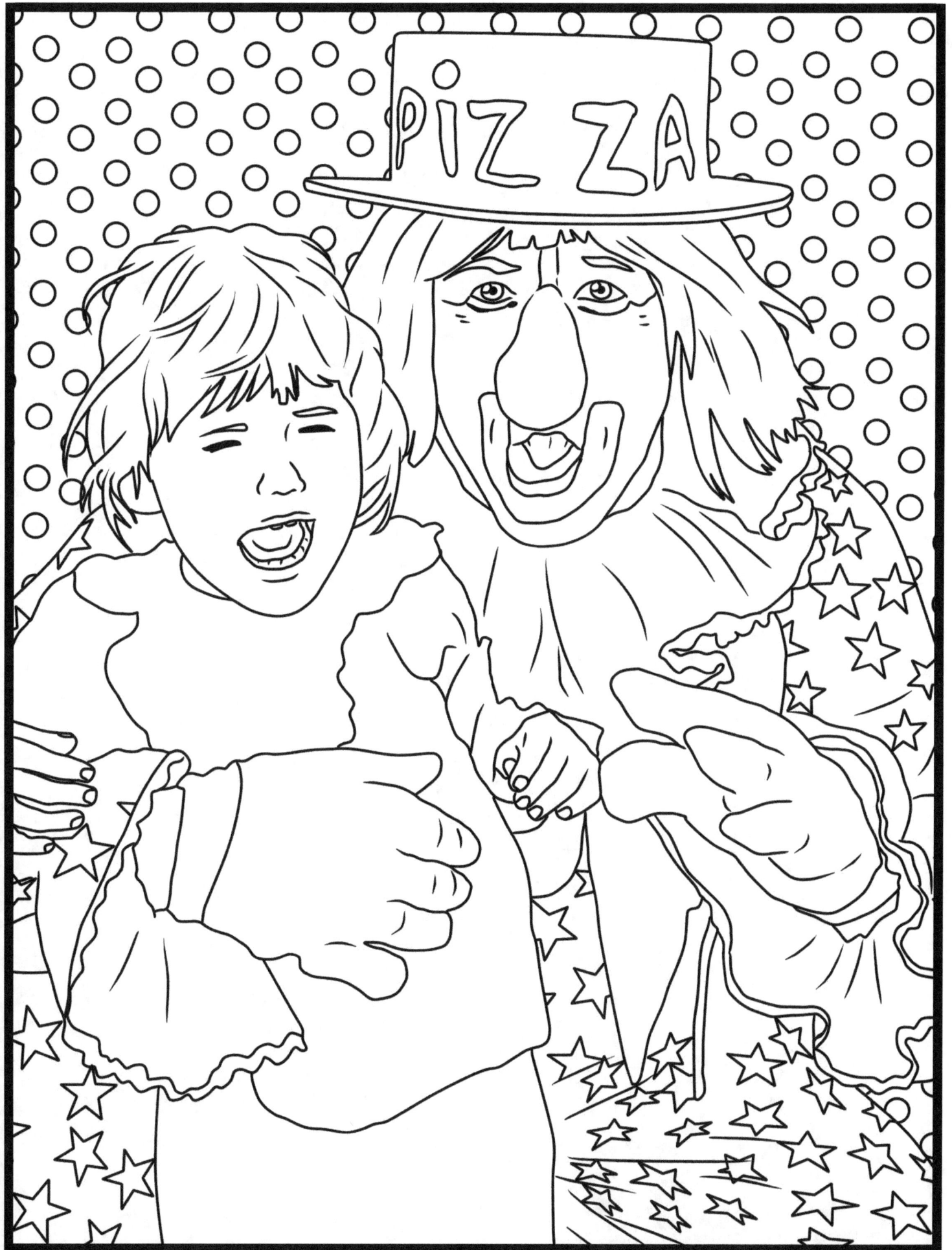

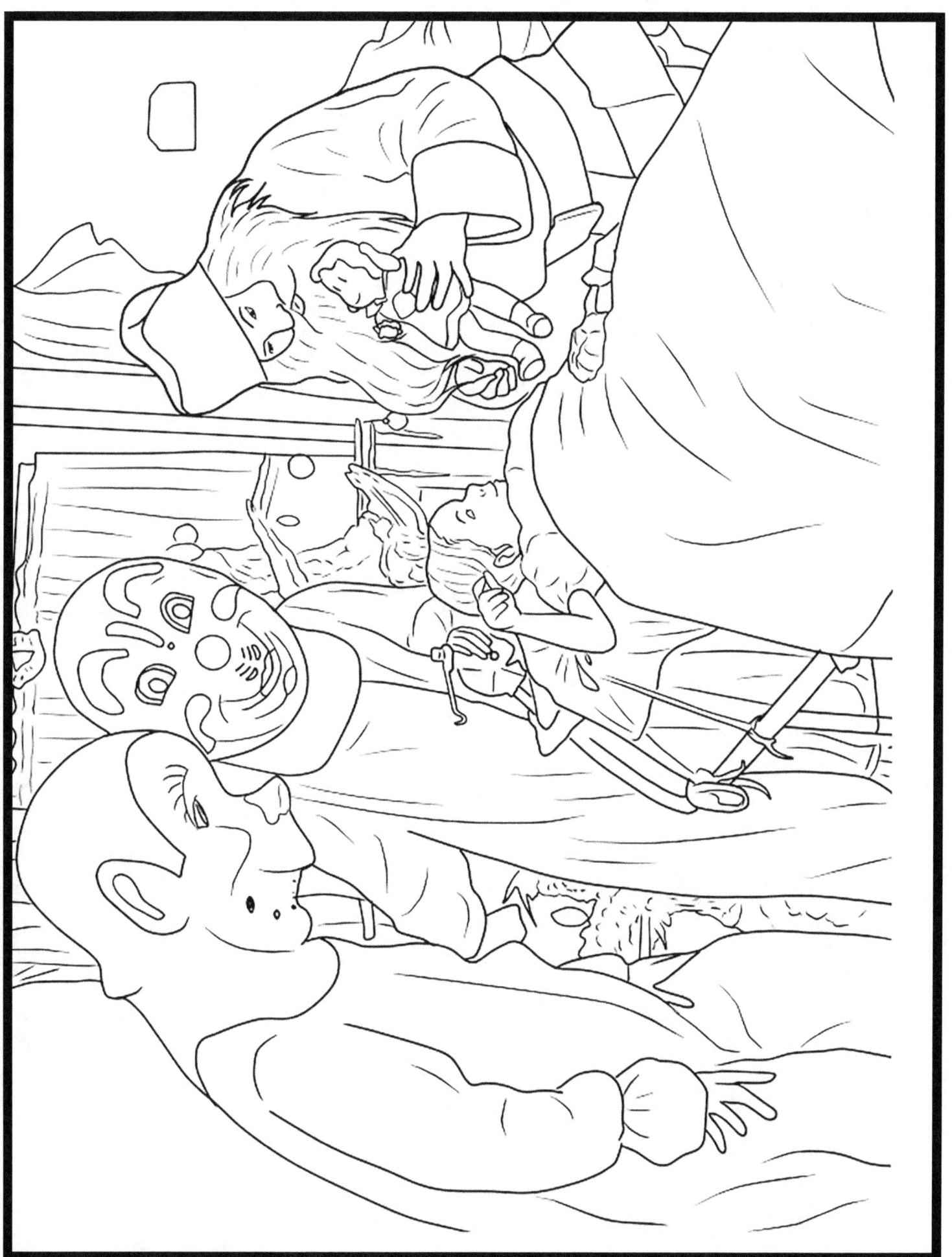

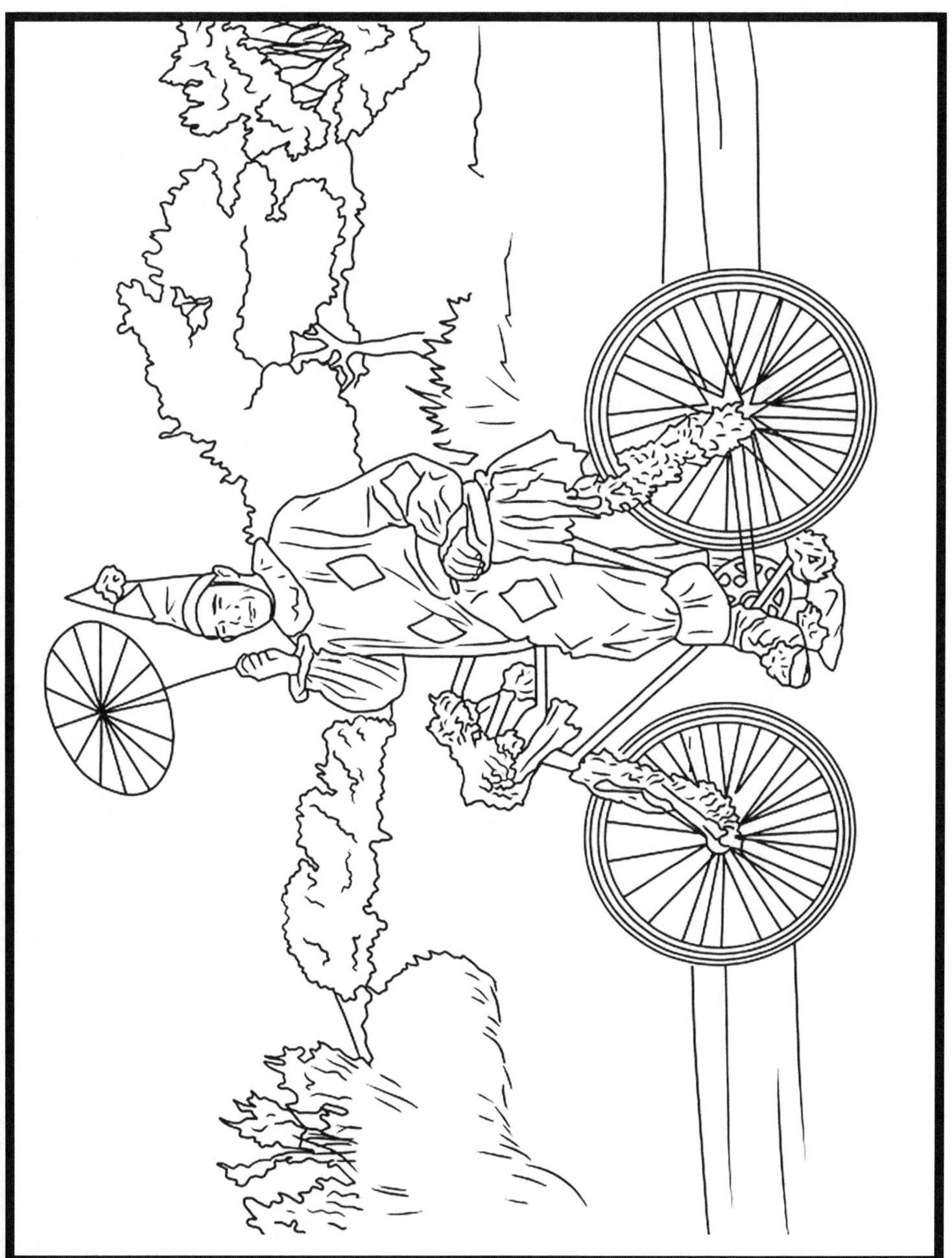

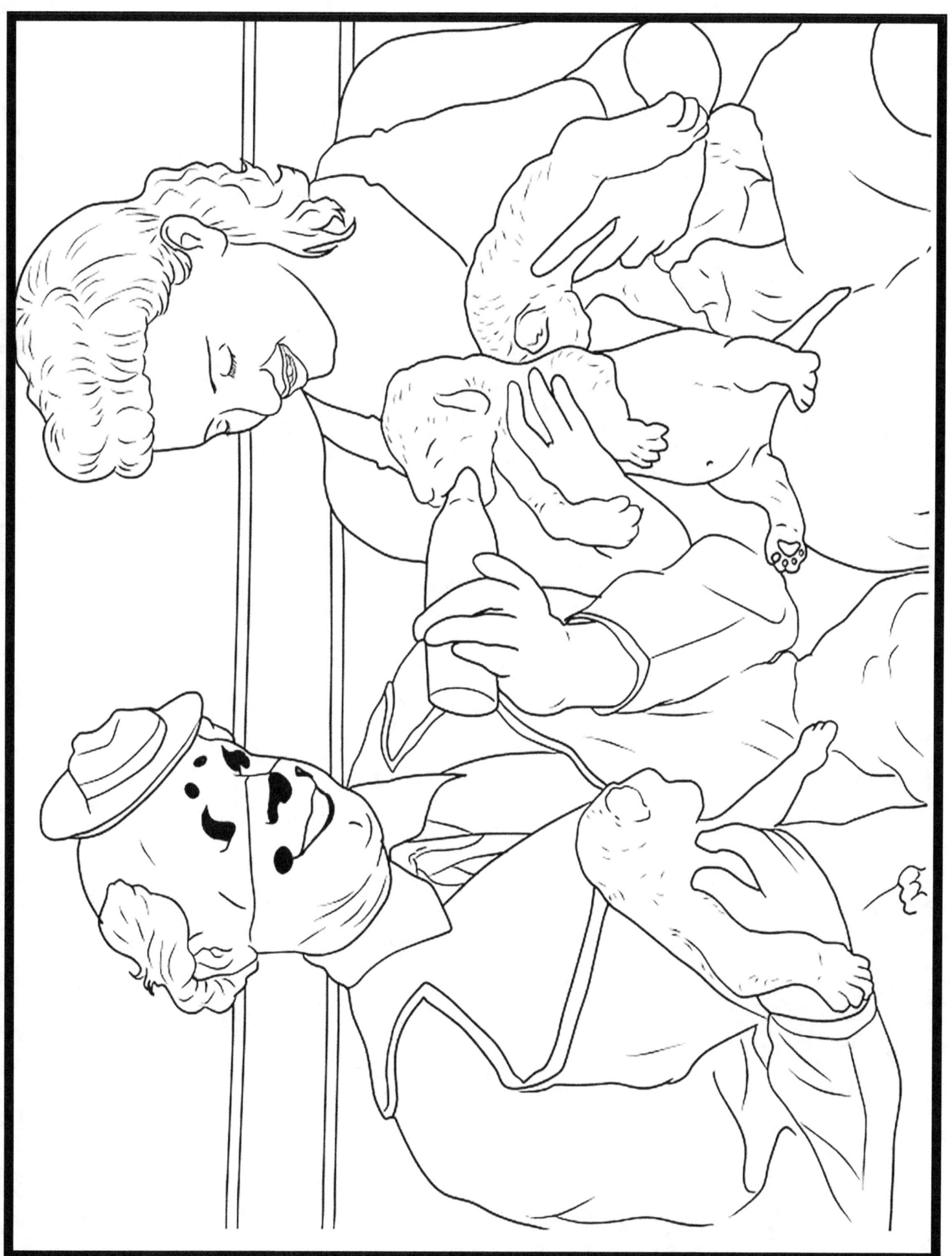

ABOUT THE AUTHOR

Jordan Colton is an avid fan of horror he currently resides in Utah with his cat and horror film collection.

You can learn more about his horrid coloring books at:

www.horridcoloringbooks.com

Also check out his other volumes:

Volume 1: The Night of the Living Dead
Volume 2: The Krampus
Volume 3 : Manos the Hands of Fate

www.ingramcontent.com/pod-product-compliance
Lightning Source LLC
Chambersburg PA
CBHW081004170526
45158CB00010B/2908